D0940700

The Sport Diver's Guide To
Sunken Treasure

By

David Finnern

PEARL PUBLISHING COMPANY

This book could never have been written without the able assistance of several individuals who unselfishly shared their time and talents so others may experience the adventure of underwater treasure hunting. I would like to thank Rosemary Anderson and the staff at People's Publishing Company, Fred Borad, Steve Lawson, Pete Matthews, Steve Mello, Bo Mulder, Mike Piantoni and Rick Rolsheim for their assistance and for the many years of friendship. I would also like to thank Linda, Wendy, Travis, Jason, Keith, Janell and Jake for their support of the project.

It is to these people and to all with the spirit of adventure and the courage to follow their dreams that this book is dedicated.

Contents

Photo: Copyright © 1990, Mike Piantoni

Introduction

Sunken treasure! The mere mention of the term conjures images of storm-tossed Spanish galleons spilling their holds on tropical reefs; of pirate ships and buried chests filled with golden doubloons and pieces of eight. We envision professional salvage divers utilizing millions of dollars worth of high-tech gear sifting through the innermost secrets of a once proud vessel.

While it's easy to allow one's imagination to run rampant with such visions, practicality soon overshadows enthusiasm as we realize we probably do not have the resources to mount a major salvage expedition. But must we really abandon the dream due to limited resources? Sunken treasure can be found in many forms for as long as mankind has ventured into the water he has left remnants of his passing. Shipwrecks are one such remnant, but certainly not the only one. And the remnants are not isolated to a century ago, but were lost yesterday as well.

There was a time I believed recovering sunken gold, silver, rubies, diamonds and artifacts was reserved for an elite few. However, I was proven wrong on my very first beach dive with a metal detector. It was early one Thanksgiving morning. The family was expected for the traditional feast that afternoon so my wife was already busy in the kitchen. Since the kitchen and I have always been mortal enemies, I left, at my wife's request, to make a dive with my new underwater metal detector.

I had purchased the detector primarily for use on shipwreck sites and gave little thought to other possibilities. I arbitrarily chose a beach to test the unit for no other reason than it was close to my home. After suiting up and a brief walk across the sand, I settled onto the bottom and switched on the machine. Within a few swings of the coil, an abundance of metal began to register. The first few targets proved to be pulltabs and bottle caps. They were worthless but I was satisfied that the detector did as it was advertised. But as I fanned the sand away from the next target, a quarter suddenly popped from the hole. It wasn't much of a treasure, but the thought that a swimmer had inadvertently lost it was intriguing none the less.

With a little more focus and deliberate searching, another target registered below the coil. I fanned the sand and soon a cone-shaped indentation formed below my hand. I swept the coil over the hole. The target still registered somewhere below so I delicately removed a little more sand. Suddenly, a flash of gold radiated from the bottom. As my hand lightly fanned, more of the yellow metal became exposed. I couldn't stand the suspense any longer and reached into the hole and retrieved a massive gold ring adorned with 11 diamonds mounted in a heart-design on top.

I was elated, but a little confused. How did such a magnificent and valuable ring come to rest below the sand? As I pondered the situation, it suddenly made perfect sense. The beach had been in use for many years. The combination of suntan lotion, swimming, the weightlessness water procures and the specific gravity of the heavy gold created a perfect scenario for lost jewelry.

With new enthusiasm and intensity, I continued searching. Coins, fishing weights and all sorts of odds and ends began filling my goody bag. Then, another flash of gold reflected from the bottom of a hole. This time a beautiful gold ring with two large diamonds and a ruby emerged from the sandy bottom.

I didn't realize it at the time, but this dive was just the beginning of an adventure that would take me to countless swimming beaches, old river ports, lake-front saloons and steamship wharves in search of lost treasure. It was merely the genesis that would ultimately lead to the discovery of old coins, gold and silver jewelry, artifacts and antique bottles, and to a life of exploration.

The purpose of this book is to share the adventure and the techniques which have proven successful. I firmly believe that anyone can experience the dream of discovering sunken treasure with a minimal investment of time and money, and by following a few simple steps.

It awaits discovery. It is to that end, this book is written.

CHAPTER 1.

Metal Detectors and Accessories

Searching for sunken treasure can be simple or complicated, expensive or inexpensive. I have known successful treasure hunters who have found thousands of dollars worth of antique bottles by merely probing the wet sand with a stick. Others prefer searching for old ports and shipwrecks with sophisticated electronic equipment in custom-made boats. For most underwater treasure hunters, however, the metal detector is the cornerstone of their equipment.

Metal detectors for water use can be categorized by two basic designs: shallow water and underwater. Shallow water detectors are primarily splash proof or, in some cases, may be guaranteed to a depth of 30 feet or so. Underwater detectors, on the other hand, are designed for diving and may be guaranteed to depths of 250 feet and more.

The waterproof integrity of a specific detector is a critical issue when choosing a unit. While an underwater detector may be used for diving, beach or shallow water hunting, a shallow water detector is limited in depth and usually not suitable for serious underwater applications.

Opinions infinitely vary as to the best detector for finding sunken treasure and it would be unfair to the reader to go into an in-depth study here since technology is ever-changing. I

Today's underwater metal detectors are both affordable and easy to operate. Fisher Research Laboratory manufactures several models within the sport diver's budget.

have personally used and field tested numerous detectors arriving at one conclusion: They all find treasure. Therefore, the criteria that should dictate an ultimate choice should be based on personal budget, projected use of the detector and where it is to be used.

As mentioned previously, the type of detector desired should initially be narrowed to shallow water or underwater which is as simple as deciding at what depth you're going to dive with the unit. However, after this decision is made, the novice maybe overwhelmed with information which can seem confusing.

Probably the first source of confusion when shopping for a detector arises from the use of acronyms. These actually appear more complex than they really are and have evolved for the simple purpose of abbreviating long strands of words that stand for relatively basic processes. A partial list of the most common abbreviations can be seen in the chart below.

VTI... Visual Target Identification
ADS...................................... Automatic Detection System
VLF/TR........ Very Low Frequency/Transmitter Receiver
AGC................................... Automatic Ground Cancel
VDI................................ Visual Discrimination Indicator
ATI.................................... Audio Target Identification
TR/DISC......... Transmitter Receiver with Discrimination
BFO...................................... Beat Frequency Oscillator
TR.. Transmitter Receiver
DISC.. Discriminator
SPD.......................... Synchronous Phase Discrimination
DS.. Deep Seeker
PI.. Pulse Induction
GBD............................ Ground Balancing Discriminator
GNC................................... Ground Neutralizing Circuit
GC... Ground Cancel
GEB..................................... Ground Exclusion Balance
GCD..................................... Ground Canceling Detector
BBS... Broad Band Spectrum

With a quick glance at the chart one realizes the first step to purchasing the right detector is education, and your local treasure hunting shop is the first place to start. A local specialist knows not only about detectors but about your specific locale. He is also prepared to show you the latest advances in detecting technology as well as tried and true favorites.

Reading is another method of education. Some treasure magazines feature metal detector field tests which address both the positive and negative aspects of a detector. Even if the test is concerning a detector that is not specifically designed for water use, it can still be a valuable source of information by addressing issues and concerns of which you should be aware. Field tests offer answers about a specific detector, but in doing so they also teach the beginning treasure hunter what questions to ask. Battery life, detector weight, coil size, depth capabilities, price, warranty, circuitry, search modes...these are topics with which one should be familiar prior to purchasing any metal detector.

Another benefit to treasure magazines is you can read about firsthand experiences of successful treasure hunts. Seek those articles which were written about the type of hunting you'll be doing, preferably in the same general geographic location. Read articles carefully and note what was found with each type of detector.

Some publications, such as *Western and Eastern Treasures* published by People's Publishing Company, list local treasure hunting clubs, dealers and upcoming events. There is nothing quite so valuable as local veterans to educate you in the requirements of your particular area. It has been my experience that treasure hunters are some of the friendliest people on earth. The mere mention that you're new to the endeavor at any club meeting should enlist ample help and invitations.

Another valuable publication is the *Treasure Hunter's Buyers Guide* also published by People's Publishing Company (P.O. Box 1598, Mercer Island, WA 98040-1598). This book outlines most detectors which are found on today's market so side-by-side comparisons can be made without traveling all over town. It is updated periodically and lists the latest treasure hunting accessories which are available as well.

Video tapes are another source of information. Many

manufacturers, distributors and dealers are producing instructional videos about a myriad of treasure hunting topics. These range from how to operate specific detectors to specialized hunting techniques.

While all this may sound complicated, it's really not. Only a relative few types of detectors work well in the water. Unlike the early BFO (beat frequency oscillator) underwater detectors, the new generation of water detectors are user friendly and relatively simple. The two types commonly used underwater are VLF/TR (very low frequency/transmitter receiver) and PI (pulse induction) machines. Both types have distinct benefits and capabilities yet differ from one another in several ways.

Pulse Induction

Pulse induction technology has a major advantage over other types of circuitry for water hunting since it ignores black sand, salt and other minerals commonly found in water. Because of this distinction, a PI detector often "punches" through mineralized sea bottoms with detection depth that is hard to beat. This is, no doubt, the reason PI detectors are the choice of so many professional underwater salvors.

PI detectors work by sending bursts of magnetic energy with alternating pauses in between. Any metallic anomaly within the sand is registered by comparing the returning signals and then relayed to the diver by either sound, lights or both.

Most PI machines are non-motion detectors. In other words, the coil need not be moving to operate properly. This makes pinpointing a target easy. It also makes PI detectors simpler to use in uneven areas, such as rock or coral reefs, where swinging a coil is difficult. Most PI machines are relatively simple to use and utilize only two or three controls for ground balancing, audio volume and on/off.

Pulse induction detectors work well for most water or beach applications but as with most everything there is a tradeoff with some machines. Many PI detectors are slow to respond electronically. This means the sweep speed must be maintained at a slightly slower rate than other types of detectors or a target may be passed over before the machine has time to respond. Another disadvantage is some PIs drain batteries relatively

The Fisher Research Laboratory "Impulse" pulse induction metal detector utilizes only two controls to operate its features.

quickly. One unit I owned went through a set of alkaline batteries in about 12 hours of operation whereas another PI machine I used worked well for 40 hours on a set of the same brand. Another concern is discrimination circuitry. PI detectors use a pulse delay process for discrimination purposes. Since this can drastically reduce the depth capabilities, many manufacturers opt not to offer the option on their PI detectors.

VLF/Discrimination

VLF/TR detectors use similar technology to that of a common radio. While more sensitive to ferrous oxides (mineralization) in water, they are extremely practical for all-around treasure hunting. Most VLF machines have a discrimination circuit which helps out in areas cluttered with

Underwater metal detectors utilizing multiple frequencies usually offer several search mode options but are slightly more complicated to use.

junk. Most water hunters use little, if any, discrimination. However, it can be a welcome addition when diving an old pier or other site which is blanketed with small nails and metal debris.

Another advantage to VLF detectors with discrimination circuitry is they can be immediately adapted to land use. I first noticed the benefit of this when surfacing from a dive at a local beach. As I loaded my equipment into my truck, I noticed the sidewalks had recently been removed for new construction. Since the area had once been an old port, I checked the dirt with my detector before driving home. And good thing I did.

The soil was littered with coins dating back to the 1870s. But it was also littered with nails and everything else imaginable so using some discrimination was imperative or I'd be digging still.

While discrimination circuitry sounds like a wonderful asset, it can also be the source of missed treasure. Setting the discrimination level to where it rejects pulltabs and bottle caps will almost ensure that coins on edge, thin gold rings, nickels and small gold coins will also be rejected. It is for this reason most water hunters use no discrimination whenever possible. And when in a situation where it is necessary to use discrimination, it should be set at a level which only rejects small nails. You might dig some junk this way, but you won't pass up that elusive gold coin either.

Multiple Frequencies

Several modern detectors utilize multiple frequencies. The thought behind this technology is the machine can adequately discriminate iron while still detecting a nonferrous target.

These detectors work well in areas littered with nails and other metal debris and several are available for underwater and shallow water applications. Another advantage to multiple frequencies is their ability to identify targets. Each type of metal gives off a different sound consequently both air and energy can be saved for only promising targets. This can indeed be an asset in trashy areas but, like discrimination circuitry, it will be the source of missed treasure if relied upon exclusively.

Probes

An electronic probe is merely a mini-detector which can be used to pinpoint a target. Some probes attach to a primary detector and utilize its discrimination and ground balance adjustments while others are independent and complete detectors. While their primary function is pinpointing, another use for this tool is crevicing around rocks where swinging a coil is impractical. Unfortunately, most probes are made to install on land detectors since the coil cords are not permanently fixed in place. However the probe itself may be submersible which makes it a handy tool for beach and shallow water hunting.

Search Coils

Search coils can be categorized by their shape and by the type of windings they employ. The two coil shapes commonly found on underwater detectors are round and elliptical (oval). Shape does not necessarily dictate the type of windings within the coil, however. Each search coil has two sets of windings. These can be in a concentric (round) design or a Double-D pattern. The concentric design consists of two circular windings, one within the other. The Double-D pattern resembles two back-to-back and narrow "Ds" with a slight space in between.

The variables in the shape and windings affect the search pattern of the coil. A round coil with concentric windings will have a cone-shaped detection pattern. This combination gives both good depth and sensitivity, but the operator must overlap his search pattern by half the coil width to ensure reading deep targets due to the cone-shaped detection pattern. The concentric windings are also very adept at discriminating iron in wet ground and are extremely sensitive to small pieces of deeply-embedded gold. This is the most common type of search coil and therefore addressed most often in this book.

An elliptical-shaped coil need not be overlapped as much since the coil is longer and thus penetrates the ground with a longer signal. This effect is magnified if the coil is equipped with Double-D windings since a narrow, rectangular signal is sent into the ground rather than cone-shaped. This means the signal length at depth is nearly the same as at the surface, but some sensitivity is lost to small pieces of gold.

Coil size is another important factor since search coils are not interchangeable on most water detectors like they are on their land counterparts. The diameter of search coils varies from about 3" to 12" for water detectors. Generally, the larger the coil, the deeper it penetrates due to the cone-shaped pattern of concentric windings. In other words, while you may be detecting a 12" sweep on the surface, you may be covering only a one inch area at an eight inch depth. For this reason,

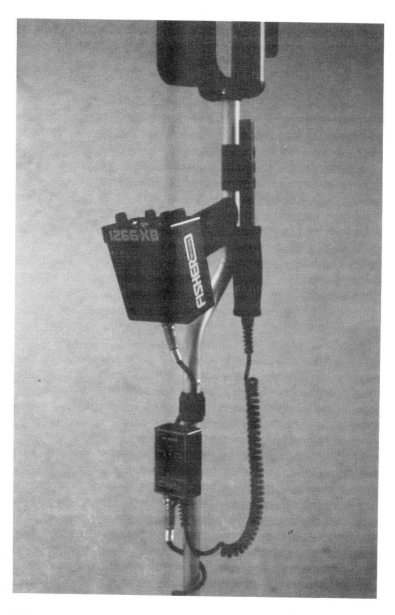

Most probes are made for land detectors, however the handle portions are usually submersible.

water hunters usually prefer a large coil when searching sandy areas.

There are several problems with a large coil in some areas, however. A larger coil can be difficult to maneuver around uneven areas simply because it cannot reach in close to crevices, coral or rocky surfaces. A larger coil is also difficult to use in areas filled with junk targets. In these trashy areas, the coil will register several targets simultaneously making pinpointing almost impossible. Even with a target ID mode, it can be difficult to isolate a promising target when several are registering concurrently. If trashy or rocky areas typify your hunting arena, a smaller coil would probably be much more productive.

The ideal setup is to have two or three detectors with different size coils. Since this is fairly costly, many underwater treasure hunters opt for an 8" coil which works well for just about all circumstances.

Batteries

Power source is another concern when purchasing a metal detector. There are three types of batteries generally used in metal detectors: alkaline, carbon-zinc and nicads. One might assume nicad batteries are the primary choice since they are rechargeable and cost effective. But there is a specific dilemma when using rechargeable batteries in some underwater detectors. Nicad batteries should be charged just prior to using them. In a land detector this is not a problem. In some water detectors, this can be a time consuming endeavor. Each time batteries are removed from a waterproof detector, the O-rings and both seats must be cleaned of sand and grit, and the O-rings greased with silicone lubricant. While it is easy to charge and install the batteries, it takes a bit of time to reseal the waterproof integrity of the machine every time it is to be used. Also, some nicad batteries can periodically develop a memory and require de-charging, thus a de-charging unit must be purchased soon after buying your detector.

For detectors in which the batteries are removed for charging or replacement, alkaline batteries may be a better choice. They last considerably longer than carbon-zinc batteries yet limit the time of dismantling, cleaning, sealing and reassembling the detector. Another advantage is it's convenient to carry an extra set of batteries when traveling or on a boat without worrying about a charging station.

Nicad batteries work extremely well in detectors which can be charged through the housing. By the mere fact they need not be removed for service, most problems are eliminated and regular battery replacement is unnecessary. Some underwater detectors are also equipped with the nicads implanted into a separate waterproof housing. In this type, several battery packs can be carried and a new set can simply be "plugged in" when needed.

To Float Or Not To Float

Buoyancy is another factor to consider when choosing a metal detector for water use. If you are going to dive with the detector, it is wise to consider if an optional weight is included or available to make it negatively buoyant. A floating detector is impractical underwater since it tends to float to the surface each time it's set aside to dig or investigate a target. Most underwater units have weights available which either insert into the shaft or clip onto the outside of the upper stem. These weights are imperative for serious underwater hunting. Keep in mind these weights should be designed to be mounted as far from the coil as possible.

Accessories

Once a detector has been purchased, a digging tool is the next piece of equipment to consider. For shallow-water hunters who wade into the water the treasure scoop is a required piece of equipment, but it is an option for divers. Scoops come in a variety of styles and are made from several different materials. Some treasure hunters prefer a plastic scoop since the detector coil can be scanned over it to see if a target has been dug and trapped inside. Others prefer steel since the shovel end is thinner making it easier to penetrate hard-packed sand or mud.

Sand scoops are available in several diameters and with a variety of handle extensions.

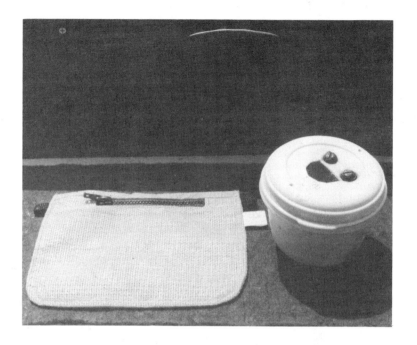

A secure enclosure is required for retaining smaller items such as rings and coins.

All scoops are designed to do one thing: sift the sand and retain the treasure. And it's been my experience that all scoops do just that. So the decision comes down to details rather than major differences. Wire mesh scoops sift much faster than those utilizing round holes. For this reason they seem to be the primary choice of most beach hunters. However, since the entire bowl is usually wire mesh, they may not last quite as long as solid steel or plastic.

Comfort is another concern when choosing a treasure scoop. There should be no sharp edges near the handle or chafing might result. A foam hand grip can also be a welcome feature after long hours of digging through the sand.

Versatility is another consideration if you plan on using the scoop for purposes other than diving. Many scoops can be used by themselves, or attached to a variety of long-handled extensions. These extensions can vary from 12" so bending is kept to a minimum when beach hunting to four or five feet for shallow-water use.

In the event hard-packed clay or gravel is encountered, a knife or trowel is probably a better choice for retrieving targets. Several commercial trowels and digging tools are manufactured specifically for treasure hunting. In most cases, a well-made diving knife or garden shovel will also suffice. The paramount feature required in a digging tool is it be made of good-quality stainless steel. Anything less will bend when first used and rust in a short time.

The next required item for underwater treasure hunting is a secure container in which to place your finds. Finding a suitable treasure container for underwater hunting is a bit more difficult than for land treasure hunting. Water tends to steal most everything. That's why water hunting is so lucrative. But without an adequate enclosure to contain your finds, our wet friend will steal that diamond ring long before you have time to surface with it.

A diver's nylon mesh goody bag works well for larger items, however it is not suitable for rings or jewelry. Smaller items require special handling. A plastic film canister works well for this purpose but is limited to the number of rings it will hold (you have to think positive). A small Tupperware container does a better job. If you want to be creative, a hole can be cut in the lid of the container and a flapper valve installed. This allows for treasure to be inserted into the Tupperware without taking off the lid. A lead fishing weight can also be added to make the container negative buoyant.

Other usable options include a small-mesh nylon bag with a zipper or a lead shot bag. These can be attached to your diving equipment or placed inside your conventional goody bag.

A few extra items can add to the success of any treasure venture. This is especially the case if travel is an integral part of your treasure hunting endeavors. A travel kit should include extra batteries, O-rings, sun block, hat, flashlight and first aid supplies. In addition to the basics, a well-equipped travel kit should include a compass, notebook, pens and pencils, zip-lock bags, coin book and, of course, a Swiss Army knife for field repairs. Another handy tool to include is a pair of

Accessories within a travel bag can make treasure hunting more enjoyable and may even save a trip from being a wasted effort.

navigation dividers. This inexpensive instrument makes it possible to walk off any scale on a map or chart to ensure you end up where you want to be. These items may very well save the day from being a wasted effort. They can also help you find or relocate the "hot spot" by using compass bearings and logging information in a notebook.

A camera and a G.P.S. (Global Positioning System) are two other items which can help in relocating a site. By taking photos of the surrounding area and landmarks, a site can again be visited by lining up on your photos. A hand-held G.P.S. is capable of pinpointing just about any area on earth by receiving multiple satellite signals. These marvelous units tell you the exact direction to travel in order to reach any destination.

In addition to a note book in the field, a permanent log book is an important asset in treasure hunting. This can be a simple three-ring binder with lined paper or something more extravagant. Information to be logged can vary, but such things as items discovered, tides, conditions, depth and time of year may ultimately show trends which can prove beneficial in planning future treasure hunts. Hand-drawn maps listing the location of finds can also help to jog the ol' memory when returning to a site.

There is another value to a log book when dealing with older finds. Any relic or artifact discovered should be treated with the utmost care and all researched information regarding the item, including the location where it was found, should be recorded. History belongs to all of us and there is a serious responsibility when you're the one discovering it. The relic you find may be yours for a time, but you are merely the caretaker. It will ultimately fall into the hands of your heirs or a museum and all pertinent information should be readily available so future generations can know and understand the story and facts behind the discovery.

The right equipment is essential to ensure success. However, the next step is to understand how, when and where to search.

CHAPTER 2.

The Basics-How, When And Where

It would seem all treasure hunters should have an equal opportunity if armed with the same equipment, but in reality nothing could be further from the truth. Some individuals consistently reap more and better finds even in "picked over" areas. The reasons for this can be attributed to three characteristics found in all successful treasure hunters. They research the site, they're prepared, and they know their equipment. So before rushing off with your new detector a few simple steps should be taken.

While metal detectors all do the same thing, they do not

accomplish the feat in the same way. Hence, the first priority in metal detecting is understanding your particular detector. The instruction manual is the first place to start. The manual must be studied and fully comprehended before leaving for the beach or local lake. This is imperative not only for successful treasure hunting but to ensure your new detector is not damaged from improper use.

Regardless of where you'll be using your detector, it is also wise to set up a mock site in the back yard or at a local beach just to see how the detector reacts to gold, silver, copper, and different types of coins. This can be accomplished by burying different items at various depths and running the coil over the test plot. The first pass over the items should be done using no discrimination and full sensitivity taking note of the sound and response each item produces. After writing down each response, increase the discrimination slightly and repeat the process. Of primary importance is the point at which the machine discriminates out small gold rings and other valuable targets. This point can be relative to the target's depth so the various items should be tested at several depths.

Sweep speed is another important factor in which experimentation is needed. The instruction manual should give information on the optimum speed in which to swing the coil. However, this is a critical factor which requires practice since smaller and deeper targets may be missed if the coil is moving too slow or too fast. When testing both speed and target response, try to locate the maximum depth penetration for different items since better targets are often found deep when hunting a wet environment.

Once competent in these areas, comfort is the next important consideration. Again, your instruction manual will give invaluable information regarding the adjustment of your detector. But each treasure hunter must find his own style and "fit" which enables him to hunt for long periods of times without exhaustion or muscle fatigue. Since numerous detectors can be adapted to hip-mounting, which drastically reduces the weight, many prefer this configuration when beach hunting. But this is not acceptable for underwater hunting since the cord can become entangled in rocks or coral.

The detector adjustment is a major factor in diving for

There are numerous ways in which to search for a treasure site including towing a diver behind a boat.

reasons other than comfort. Usually, the shafts should be compacted as close as possible when using a metal detector underwater. Swinging a coil extended four feet is both tiresome and ineffective underwater. Since visibility is usually limited near the beach, extended shafts also make it difficult to locate what the coil has discovered. While there's some concern a short shaft configuration may cause the detector to react to the diver's equipment, the risk is minimal; and if the problem does arise, it can be corrected by holding the detector farther from your body.

Adjusting the shaft in its most compact form can cause a minor problem with extra cord. Under no circumstances should a diver venture into the water with extra cord waving in the swell due to the danger of it becoming entangled. Always wind the extra coil cord around the shaft until it's neatly stored, but allow some play at the coil and where it connects to the control box to prevent stress on the connections.

The Search

Once you're comfortable with the detector and its controls, it's time to hit the water. Hunting in and around water is slightly different than hunting land sites. First, you should assume targets are deeply embedded. This means your sweep speed and technique should be specifically adapted for deep targets. And it means you should always begin your search using maximum sensitivity and no discrimination whenever possible to assure maximum depth.

As previously mentioned, most search coils have a cone-shaped detection pattern. To search an area effectively, the search pattern must overlap at least half the coil width. This is probably the most common error committed by underwater treasure hunters. It is also the reason so many treasure hunters find newer quarters in abundance, but gold rings and older coins elude them.

A graphic example of this occurred while I was beach hunting after a storm. I noticed foot prints and coil marks in the area I wanted to hunt. I also noticed the footprints were spaced about three feet apart indicating my predecessor had gone through the area extremely fast. I began searching in his path and, predictably, discovered a man's gold ring directly under a footprint.

Another common error is swinging the coil too far above the sand. Detecting deep targets requires the coil be close to or on the sand. There is no reason to position the coil an additional four or five inches above the sand which ensures many targets will be missed. Most treasure hunters do not purposely position the coil too high. The cause is usually holding the coil at an angle or, more likely, swinging the coil upward at the end of each sweep. The best technique always includes making a conscious effort to keep the coil close and parallel to the bottom at all times.

When starting out, there seems to be a natural tendency to be excited over large and loud targets. However, gold rings, chains, bracelets and pendants can be very small indeed and

Gold rings, such as these found at swimming beaches, usually sink deep into the sand.

may give off minimal response. And a very small ring can hold a vary large diamond. It is the whisper, the wisp of sound barely discernible that usually indicates true treasure. For this reason the volume must be turned high enough to hear faint sounds even through a wetsuit hood, and concentration is an absolute must or valuable targets will surely be missed.

Once a target has been detected, it must be pinpointed prior to digging. The easiest way to pinpoint a target is by simply drawing an "X" with the detector's coil. To do this, move the coil forward and backward to narrow the target's position, then side to side. The target should lie in the center of the "X." I use the word "should" because a tilted coin or ring may give a signal slightly off-center so care should be the operative word in pinpointing and recovery.

Occasionally, pinpointing is difficult on an exceptionally large or shallow target. In this case try lifting the coil, raising the discrimination level or reducing the sensitivity then repeating the "X" process.

Recovering Targets

After a bit of practice, the approximate depth of a target can usually be determined by the sound of your detector. This can be deceiving since a ring at the surface may produce a similar sound to a can buried a foot or more. But generally, you'll get a feel for how your detector reacts to different targets at various depths. The importance of this relates to how a target is recovered. If a target is deep, it's much faster to remove a fair amount of sand, then check the hole with the coil and repeat the process if the target still registers. When the target no longer registers in the hole, simply run the coil over the tailings then sift out the target. It's prudent to widen the hole as it gets deeper for two reason: sand caves in fairly easily, and sometimes the target is off to one side.

There are three basic techniques in underwater target recovery. The easiest method is to simply fan the sand away from you. This is accomplished by waving a gloved hand near the sand in a circular fashion making sure your hand returns high enough to avoid fanning the sand back into the hole. Pumping your hand up and down on the bottom is another method which works well in hard-packed sand or gravel. This loosens the sand better than just fanning it away from you. A scoop or trowel can also be used. These tools are especially useful when the bottom consists of rocks or shells. But regardless of the technique utilized, it's still easier to concentrate on removing the target from the hole then sifting through the tailings.

One device which can aid in fanning sand is the conventional ping pong paddle. Some adaptations can be made by attaching a lanyard and giving it several coats of varnish. But other than that, the ping pong paddle works well for moving sand in quantity.

This solid gold medal was recovered in only six feet of water at a popular swimming beach.

Gloves are an integral ingredient in target recovery for both health and success. The bottoms of lakes and beaches are often cluttered with broken glass, shells and razor-sharp metal debris. The thought of reaching into the mud or sand with an unprotected hand is foolish at best.

Where To Search

Once you've mastered your detector and recovery techniques, the next question is where to look. Most geographic locales have ample ocean, lake, pond or river swimming beaches; and each one is a potential site for lost coins and jewelry. The easiest place to start is the very beach you drive to with the family on those hot summer days. By the mere fact you choose this beach probably indicates many others have

Old newspapers can be an invaluable source of treasure leads.

done so as well.

Contemporary coins and jewelry are waiting below the sand at every popular beach. It might take a bit of searching, but it's been my experience that all beaches have claimed lost valuables. The primary factors that should be considered when selecting sites are popularity and age. If a beach is littered with swimmers and sunbathers every summer day it will more than likely be littered with modern coins and jewelry as well. If the beach has been in use for 100 years or more, there is a fair possibility older finds will be recovered in addition to the more modern ones.

Older beaches can be located by several research techniques. One of the most obvious and beneficial resources is local senior citizens. Many seniors can relate stories of family picnics or summer lifeguard jobs they had long ago that can lead directly to sites which may or may not still be in use. Local newspapers are another informative source. Many libraries have older newspapers on microfilm. It's a simple and fascinating process to search through old news stories about Fourth of July and other holiday celebrations occurring during the turn of the century.

Newspapers can reveal other clues to treasure as well. A local river might have had an old landing or a lake may have had an amusement pier on the site of a popular, contemporary swimming beach. Antiquated newspaper advertisements can often bring these sites to light.

Old maps are another source of useful information. Road or insurance maps of yesteryear can reveal numerous facts which are of value to the treasure hunter. Old dumps, fair grounds, schools, saloons or any structure near a river or beach probably means countless items lay just offshore.

Bottom Types

With minimal research, countless convenient sites should come to mind. But in an effort to narrow the list, another criteria can be interjected: the type of bottom. Sand is probably the most common substrate found at swimming beaches but mud, clay, gravel, rock and shell bottoms can also be frequently encountered. The type of beach or bottom will influence the amount of success that can be expected. Sand will tend hold a gold ring near the surface for a short time. But as the tide comes in and swimmers frolic, it will usually work its way down until it ultimately hits a firmer surface. Due to a less specific gravity, coins and silver fare better but still seem to work deeper with each passing day.

A rule of thumb which applies to sand is the lighter in color the sand, the more apt a target is to sink deeper. Often, sand is layered in various shades and colors and while the light beige sand on top may contain few targets, the gray, brown or black sand below may very well be filled with goodies.

While some types of sand seem to ingest coins and jewelry, most items will come to rest near the surface on gravel or rock bottoms. But because of the uneven surface, targets may very well lie at an angle and give an odd or "clipped" response from your detector. For this reason, rocky bottoms must be searched slowly and methodically.

Hard clay bottoms are fairly easy to search. I've found century old coins lying in plain view on clay surfaces. Mud bottoms, such as those found in many lakes, are by far the most difficult to search. A rule of thumb is if you can penetrate the mud with your hand up to your elbow, go find another beach.

Identifying the substrate isn't always easy or consistent since many bottoms are a combination of surfaces. Material of like weight and specific gravity will be found in layers with the lightest on top. It's not unusual to find a sand layer covering gravel which in turn covers clay, which covers bedrock. While the goodies might penetrate the sand there should be numerous coins and other items within the gravel and most certainly above the clay. No item can penetrate bedrock. The most lucrative areas to search when bedrock is encountered are the natural cracks and crevices which are usually filled with debris.

When To Search

Because of the various conditions commonly encountered, when to search is just as important as where to search. Since many swimming beaches are fairly shallow, the first rule in underwater treasure hunting is search at high water. There is nothing quite so difficult as diving in four feet of water since you're at the mercy of any surge or water movement and have to fight for negative buoyancy. Try to have at least six feet of depth when diving. It makes it easier to dig and limits your body movement when excavating due to increased negative buoyancy. In fresh water, this may mean scheduling treasure hunting in conjunction with the local dam schedule. In salt water, it always means checking the local tides for the perfect time of day.

TIDES

In the ocean, there are four daily tides approximately six hours apart. Tides do not go "in and out" as commonly presumed but rather "up and down" as a result of the sun and moon's gravitational pull. In essence, the earth is never round but egg-shaped as these forces pull the oceans in an ever-

Successful underwater metal detecting can depend on choosing the right time and conditions. (Photo Copyright 1990, Mike Piantoni)

moving rhythm. While it's true there are both high and low tides each day, the cycle can be further broken down into four distinct water levels: high-high, low-high, high-low and low-low tides. In other words, there are two high tides and two low tides. The best time for diving is usually at high tide or during an incoming high tide.

While ocean beaches are always affected by tides, rivers and adjacent lakes may also be influenced by the ocean. In this scenario, the same tidal cycles can be applied to the inland waterway, however time adjustments must be computed to allow for distance.

The easiest way to keep track of tide changes is with a tide book or calendar. Many marine hardware stores, dive shops, surf shops and tackle stores offer compact tide booklets free of charge or for a nominal fee. More detailed calendars and books are also available which may contain other pertinent local information.

There are numerous other ways to keep track of ocean and water conditions. Many local lifeguard departments have daily recorded phone messages which list tides, surf and wind conditions, air and water visibility, etc. Also, the National Weather Service has local phone numbers and radio broadcasts which may be consulted prior to driving to the beach. N.O.A.A. (National Oceanic and Atmospheric Administration) has recorded ocean and beach conditions available 24 hours a day on VHF marine radio as well.

SURF

While the tide level is an important factor in ocean treasure hunting, it is by no means the only one. Surf is both a formidable adversary and a treasure hunter's best friend. Waves are capable of removing tons of sand from a beach exposing a plethora of jewelry and coins in the process.

Waves are caused by wind and storms sometimes thousands of miles from the beach on which they ultimately collide. Since a specific stimulus caused their formation, waves travel in a specific direction. Swell direction is dictated by the direction from which the waves are generated. If the waves are traveling east, it is a west swell. If they are heading due north, it is considered a south swell.

Swell direction can be invaluable information to the water treasure hunter. If a beach faces due west, and it gets hit with a strong south swell, chances are pretty good some sand erosion will take place since the waves will be hitting the beach at an angle. In some instances, swells will attack a beach from two or more directions causing a "confused" sea, and serious sand removal.

Other ocean facts can be pertinent in addition to swell direction. Waves vary a great deal in size. But they also vary in steepness and in the intervals they're spaced. If a normal surf report reads, "West swell, two-three feet, 12 second intervals", it means the waves are coming from the west at about two-three feet high (measured from the trough to the crest of the wave), and the waves are spaced about 12 seconds apart. This would be pretty benign conditions for a west-facing beach. But if a storm blows, the surf report might change to, "South swell, six-eight feet, six second intervals." Because of the increased size, the waves will more than likely be steeper causing sand erosion with each pounding. This is especially true if an on-shore wind accompanies the storm. In addition, the close intervals of the waves pummeling the beach almost ensure massive amounts of sand will be washed out to sea leaving large cutouts (sand cliffs) at the high tide line and possibly underwater.

Unfortunately, there is another factor which should be considered before making a final decision on a beach or any site: pollution. Many bays, estuaries, rivers and other water sites are unsafe for swimming. This can be from biological or chemical pollution but in either event local lifeguard departments should be consulted before venturing into an unknown body of water. It is also a sound practice to avoid diving around drainage pipes or sewage outfalls, especially after a rain storm.

Once a beach has been selected, one point to keep in mind is most beachgoers don't swim, they wade. This places the vast majority of lost goodies in relatively shallow water, probably five to 12 feet at high tide. As every beach diver knows, most ocean beaches are plagued by the relentless back and forth water movement called surge. Even moderate surge makes diving with a detector difficult and relocating a target almost impossible. If the surge or swell is formidable there is no reason to go into the water for it will be almost impossible to find treasure.

By monitoring sea conditions, a beach can be chosen based on facts rather than arbitrary guess work. When this knowledge is coupled with treasure hunting skill and competence, lucrative and productive hunting is almost assured.

Various items can be found with a metal detector including antique tokens and foreign coins.

Specialized Equipment

In addition to basic treasure hunting knowledge, specialized diving equipment and techniques can also aid in discovering sunken treasure. For many types of diving, a downline is a useful piece of equipment, but it is often imperative in many types of underwater treasure hunting discussed in this book.

A downline is simply a rope anchored to the bottom and buoyed at the surface which is used as a reference point. When diving from a boat, the anchor line is usually utilized for this purpose. When beach diving, a diving float with diver's flag should be used. Three things should be kept in mind when choosing a downline: it should be visible in limited conditions, it should be long enough to allow for incoming tides or rising water, and a diver down flag should be attached to the end. Yellow polypropolene line works well for this purpose. It floats therefore extra line does not collect on the bottom and entangle the diver. It is relatively impervious to sun and water damage. And the yellow color is fairly visible underwater.

To eliminate storing and unwinding massive amounts of line, it's advisable to make several sections of line with a loop on one end and a brass clip on the other end of each section. In this way, a shallow dive is not encumbered with 100 feet of extra line floating about yet the various sections can easily be attached together if more line is needed.

The weight required to anchor the downline is somewhat relative to the wind, currents and depth. For most areas, a four pound lead diving weight will do the job. In more extreme conditions, a small boat anchor would be advisable.

The float should be a standard diver's float with an attached diver's flag mounted on a three foot staff. In areas where boat traffic is an impossibility, such as roped swimming beaches, almost any floating device will work. In these confined areas, commercial plastic buoys work well for a downline float but if budget is a major concern, a yellow plastic mustard container (less mustard) or a plastic milk container (I won't say it) will suffice.

A standard diver's buoy with flag is required in most circumstances.

Another line is required in deep or limited visibility diving, or where there is any possibility of a submerged or floating structure which could impede the diver's safe ascent. The most efficient device for a search pattern or to lead your way back to the downline is a wreck/cave diver's reel. These reels contain about 300 feet of line stored on a compact reel. Once attached to the downline, it is easy to pay out the line when searching and just as easy to wind it back on the spool when returning to the downline. There is another distinct advantage to using a reel and surfacing on a downline. For reasons unknown to the author, the average boat operator has no clue what a diver's or alpha flag means. Surfacing in open water can indeed be a dangerous endeavor. This is especially true if jet skiers are prevalent in the area.

A diving reel is a necessity in some conditions.

Training

A well-equipped diver is nothing without proper training. It goes without saying that basic certification is required to treasure hunt with scuba equipment, and many types of underwater treasure hunting can be performed with a mere fundamental understanding of diving. But some types of underwater treasure hunting require more than basic certification. Deep, wreck, and limited visibility diving are just three examples of underwater exploration which require advanced and/or specialty diver ratings.

Underwater treasure hunting requires a diver be comfortable in the wet environment and diving skills must be honed until they are second nature. After all, one cannot find treasure if all effort is expended trying to survive. For this reason, there simply is no substitute for experience and advanced or higher certification.

Attitude

There is one other consistent attribute found in most successful treasure hunters, one which is difficult if not impossible to articulate. Some treasure hunters subscribe to the notion that treasure can be found by long-range locators, map dowsing, and any number of metaphysical phenomenon. While I am personally skeptical, I do believe that proper attitude can play an important role in any endeavor and treasure hunting is no exception.

It is curious that most people find exactly what they're looking for. While I suppose this concept can be applied to life in general, it definitely applies to the art of treasure hunting. Treasure diver Steve Mello described it this way: "Watch people collecting shells on the beach. They'll pass right by an exposed coin or ring. They don't even see it. Yet the next pretty shell within 20 feet, however obscure, will not escape their attention."

This is an important factor in underwater treasure hunting. We can become so absorbed when looking for coins that we miss the antiquated bottle. Or, we can be so caught-up in searching for something big, we can't see the small gold coin. I can think of no hard and fast rules to attain the proper mental state for underwater treasure hunting. But it is wise indeed to spend a little time training your eyes to see the subtle and out-of-place straight line or the change in texture of the bottom; and to recognize treasure in all its forms and to expect the unexpected and serendipitous discovery.

Treasure can come in many forms. A treasure hunter must learn to recognize all the signs of man-made objects under the water.

39.

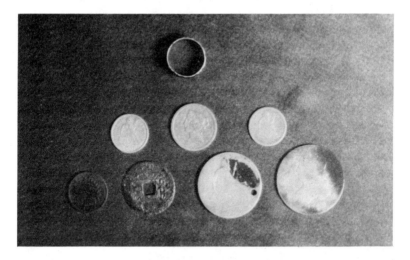

Research is the key to metal detecting beaches. These silver dollars were found at a beach where a casino once stood. The site of an over-the-water saloon yielded a $5 gold piece and coins dating back to the mid-1850s.

CHAPTER 3.

Hunting Swimming Beaches

Most certainly, swimming beaches rate as some of the more lucrative sites to hunt underwater. The primary reason for this is the reasonable expectation of finding jewelry and older coins, some of which may be extremely valuable.

For the most part, salt and fresh water beaches can be hunted in much the same manner, however individual beaches can vary a great deal and the first challenge in treasure hunting is where to start the search. The decision is relatively simple on a small lake beach since most people swim in the same vicinity and currents, which can shift the bottom and move valuables, are typically nonexistent. On a large expanse of beach, however, the choice may not be as easy.

It is usually best to begin a dive in the most popular area such as in front of the parking lot or concession stands. But since most treasure hunters prefer to dive a beach when it is relatively vacant, knowing the most vital swimming area may not be so obvious when people are absent. Therefore, a trip to the beach on a hot afternoon prior to diving may reveal a lot of information as to the most popular areas used by beachgoers. It is wise to take notes as to landmarks along the coast since

Typical finds from older beaches include Standing Liberty quarters, Barber dimes and quarters, Walking Liberty half dollars and Wheat cents.

swimmers will no longer mark the area when the beach is empty. Also make notes regarding how far out most people congregate. Since water levels can vary, it is difficult to use the surf line or water's edge for this purpose but pier pilings, a rock jetty or any other structure extending into the water will work well for a line up.

While the most populous area is a good starting point for a dive, it is not necessarily the best area for treasure hunting. After entering the water, the next task is to locate the hot spot, assuming there is one. It is a curious phenomenon but goodies of like specific gravity often collect in lines parallel to the

Though items such as keys, costume jewelry, pocket knives and inexpensive watches are worthless, they indicate the area where more valuable items may be found.

shore. Even gold can travel and change location from where it was originally lost. One way to search for a "treasure line" is to begin a dive swimming out at a 45° angle to the shore, then return to shore 90° from your original heading. With this zig-zag course you can adequately search for the proper distance out from the water's edge as well as lengthwise to the shoreline. This can be done relatively fast, but as soon as the coil begins to register keys, coins, hair pins, etc., slow down--you're there.

Once these little man-made tidbits are discovered, you know you're at the location where swimmers have inadvertently lost metal items or at least where they ultimately settled. From this point, it's best to begin to search slowly and methodically swimming parallel to shore to see if there is a line of lost valuables. A compass can be used to maintain an exact course. Ripples in the sand can also be used since they always (well, almost always) run parallel to the coast. One note: if you're following a line filled exclusively with pulltabs and pieces of aluminum, you need to travel farther in or out. There may be gold there but it is likely too deep to register.

Often when searching for a "treasure line" an underwater cutout is discovered. This is especially true when searching ocean beaches. A cutout is merely a valley or small cliff which has been created by currents or surf. They almost always run parallel to the shoreline just like any other "treasure line." These cutouts are usually very productive areas since the lighter sand has been removed along with the lighter metals and debris. This leaves gold, silver and older relics close to the surface and sometimes in abundance.

Cutouts on the beach indicate a massive amount of sand has been removed.

When a cutout is discovered, it is always prudent to carefully search the lowest part and the edges before continuing any other search pattern. Since the lighter sand has been removed exposing black mineralized sand, re-tuning your detector may be necessary to adequately detect the lowest portion of a cutout.

While it would be wonderful if there were fail-safe rules in treasure hunting, there are several exceptions to this "treasure line" rule. The dispersal area for currents in a cove is generally straight out from the center. This means that lost goodies may tend to move toward the center of the cove then travel outward. In this case a search in the center of the cove is warranted.

There is one other exception to this rule. Many of your spectacular finds won't follow any rules, so be careful of getting locked-in to any specific theory. I once found a beautiful gold and diamond engagement ring in an area filled with pulltabs. The pulltabs were actually deeper in the sand than the ring despite its heavier weight. On another occasion I was diving an old pier in a lake and found several Indian Head cents resting above new Memorial pennies...go figure!

Another important factor in beach hunting is finding specific attractions that may be present at or near the beach. These attractions include rope swings, hot springs, a cliff or diving board, or any other item which has attracted swimmers to a specific area. Often these little attractions are known only by locals or may no longer exist so some research may be needed, but it can be well worth the effort.

I located one such place simply by overhearing a conversation in which two college students discussed a cliff off which "everyone" leaped. After a few interviews with some local residents and a little research, I soon learned it was known as the ultimate challenge for cliff-leaping aficionados, the more adventurous of which rarely wore swimming trunks.

It wasn't long before I was pulling my boat into the canyon to see if the stories were true. And sure enough, the first dive proved my research correct as swimming trunks and bathing suits littered the entire area. (I'm not sure whether these were lost on impact or cast off during the flight; in either event the idea didn't seem too entertaining).

Detecting below the cliff was a tedious endeavor since

Older swimming beaches usually surrender a variety of coins and other objects such as tokens, luggage tags and watch fobs

The cliff directly behind the inflatable boat was identified as the
one which lured "leapers" from around the state. (Photo-
Western and Eastern Treasures)

The first few dives below the cliff netted numerous coins and gold and silver rings. (Photo-Western and Eastern Treasures)

remnants of the source of the leapers' courage (beer cans) blanketed the area. It soon became easier to collect the cans and remove them, then detect. The first few dives produced several gold and silver rings some of which rested on rocks in plain view. One crevice in the rock bottom was literally filled with coins. Unfortunately, none were old or silver but money is always fun to find especially when found in abundance.

Subsequent dives proved the area to be a party place for summer crowds. Small beaches in the same canyon also proved to be lucrative although hunting was slow since the entire cove was filled with cans and every type of debris imaginable.

Benches or rest areas near beaches are another intriguing area for coins. I once was diving a small bay beach and having only mediocre luck. Suddenly, I blundered into an area where coins were scattered everywhere. The majority were Wheat

Beaches can provide the treasure hunter with almost anything imaginable as evidenced by an antique toy gun, glass stoppers, silver baby spoon and other odds and ends discovered while metal detecting underwater.

One pocket located by the author surrendered numerous gold and silver necklaces, bracelets, coins and rings, a few of which are displayed above.

cents from the 1920s-1940s but an ample supply of dimes, quarters and half-dollars from the same era were also present.

Upon surfacing, I checked out the area adjacent to the underwater site. An antiquated sea wall supported a newer sidewalk on a conspicuous land protrusion into the bay. With a little research I learned a bench was once constructed there having been torn down when the new sidewalk was built. Apparently, people just couldn't help tossing a coin or two into the water as they rested on the bench.

In addition to treasure lines and specific attractions, pockets of treasure may also exist at a swimming beach.

Occasionally, one will find a small area that has been collecting coins and jewelry for 100 years or more. This is the treasure hunter's version of the prospector's "Mother Lode." I was fortunate in finding such a place. The area measured only about 6' X 12' yet was filled with rings, bracelets, medals, pendants, necklaces, and coins dating back to the late 1800s. I worked the area for about two weeks and each dive provided what seemed like an endless supply of goodies. Jack London's "Mr. Pocket" does, in fact, exist. But to ensure a pocket isn't missed, it is imperative to always check both the tailings and excavation with the search coil after retrieving a target just to make sure there aren't multiple targets in the same hole.

There is another important factor concerning the possible location of pockets. Rocks, either exposed or buried within the sand, can cause a suction behind them when a current is running much the same way as riffle bars in a sluice box. It is always prudent to search around rocks with great care. Check each fissure with the detector coil and even remove some sand around the rock to make sure multiple targets aren't somewhere below deep sand.

In addition to pockets and lines, treasure may also be located in layers. This is especially the case in older, fresh water swimming holes. One treasure hunter discovered this while diving a lake in front of an antiquated and abandoned resort. He was finding numerous relics from swimmers of yesteryear and worked the area until he felt it was cleaned out. But just as he was about to search for a new site, the thought occurred to him that just maybe older items were deeper in the gravel just beyond the scope of his metal detector.

He dug a trench about a foot deep, waited for the water visibility to clear, then made a dive with his detector. Immediately, countless items began to register at the bottom of the trench, all of which were about 20 years older than his previous finds. He continued this for some time until he had searched three generations of trenches. Each trench was about a foot deeper than the previous one, and each surrendered artifacts older than the previous trench.

Some treasure hunters prefer to hunt only trenched bottoms in the belief that most valuables lay too deep for a detector. While this philosophy is a bit too generalized for me, there is indeed reason to believe countless targets rest in deep sand or gravel. Excavation is discussed in a later chapter.

51.

Saving all items found beneath the water for later evaluation is a good habit to adopt since some antique bottles and plates are worth much more than gold or silver.

When diving a swimming beach, or just about anywhere, there is a rule which applies without exception: Save all the targets recovered whether or not they're recognizable. This makes sense for three reasons. First, there is no point in leaving a piece of junk lay on the bottom once it has been excavated. The world has enough junk laying around and we might as well clean up the trash since we went to all the work of digging it. Second, it is a bad habit to waste air and time trying to determine the identification of a target underwater. It is certainly tempting to determine a coin's date or chip away at an unrecognizable piece of conglomerate as soon as it's uncovered. However, time is limited and precious underwater, and it is much more productive to investigate the discovery on the surface. Third, water, especially salt water, can do strange things to lost items. The piece of junk you leave on the bottom may very well be a valuable find when cleaned.

A graphic example of this latter point occurred while hunting a local beach one morning. I detected a fairly deep target but, to my dismay, digging produced nothing but a hot rock (a rock which contains enough minerals to register as iron). I left the rock and continued my search, but something in the back of my mind wouldn't let go of that clump. And so, I dug the target again just to take a closer look.

It turned out this was a good move. As I examined the piece I noticed three distinct protrusions. A little rubbing with my gloved hand proved the appendages were half-embedded copper coins. I had dived enough shipwrecks to know that it wasn't a rock at all. Salt water reduces steel to a concretion which looks much like a rock.

An X-ray confirmed a total of nine coins were trapped within the conglomerate. How did they get there? Numerous theories exist. Since there is a shipwreck nearby, it may be a piece of steel that came to rest next to a lost coin purse. The salt water and years did the rest.

Regardless of where you search, just about all popular swimming beaches are loaded with gold, silver, diamonds, rubies, and coins. The question is not if it's there. The question is how to retrieve it. While finding an exact formula or strategy for searching beaches is impossible, there is one secret to success: The one who dives and digs the most, finds the most treasure. There can be frustrating times when dives produce nothing of intrinsic value. There may be times when a popular swimming beach consistently produces nothing but trash. But don't give up. If people have been using that beach, it's an absolute fact that there's gold and silver somewhere out there. It may take a winter storm to sweep the sand away or it may take more exploration. But it's out there. And it's waiting for those with the patience and perseverance to find it.

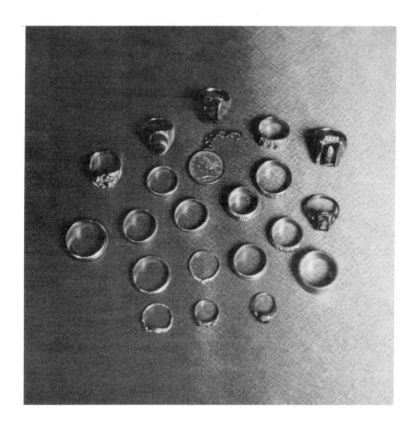

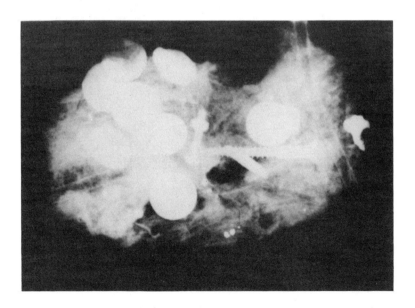

A rock? An X-ray confirmed the metal concretion contained nine coins. (Photo-Western and Eastern Treasures)

Modern swimming docks often provide contemporary jewelry such as the gold ring this diver found.

CHAPTER 4.

Diving Underwater Structures

Swimming beaches are certainly a productive locale for treasure diving. However, sooner or later many underwater TH'ers find themselves searching an underwater structure for that special relic or piece of jewelry. Old landings, docks and piers hold a special fascination for divers and may very well hold a plethora of valuables as well.

The type of treasure discovered around docks is somewhat relative to the structure's original use. Swimming docks are generally a good source of coins and jewelry lost accidentally. Old piers and wharves, on the other hand, may provide numerous items which were cast into the water intentionally such as bottles, china, and damaged ship parts. At the time of discard these items were merely considered trash but now may have extreme value as antiques.

Because it is possible to find almost anything at an old pier site, these rate as one of my personal favorite dive destinations. I have found some of my oldest coins at old docks in addition to bottles, steamship china, luggage tags, tokens...the list is endless.

There are several ways to approach diving a wharf or dock. Metal detecting can be extremely lucrative because, like most other sites, metal objects tend to sink into the sand and are out

Most anything can be found at older steamship wharves. These bottles, coins, tokens, ash trays, pocket watches, etc. were all found at one pier.

of sight. But unlike swimming beaches it's surprising how many items can be completely visible, or at least partially exposed, at these sites. Bottles and china can sometimes blanket the bottom below a wharf in full view.

Because of this, many treasure hunters are quite successful just combing the bottom looking for the exposed goodies, and this is probably the best approach when first diving a site. When visually searching, all peculiarities should be investigated since some items may appear to be a mere bump in the sand. Also, you should fan a few test holes since many objects may be hidden just below the surface of the bottom.

It is difficult to know why some items come to rest above the bottom while other like objects sink, but objects do move around the bottom so some fanning or excavation is usually necessary to reach the majority of awaiting treasures. When fanning for buried objects, it's advantageous to pay particular attention to areas around pilings or rocks. Objects, such as bottles, seem to roll around the bottom until something stops them, and often that is where they'll stay until they're discovered. While fanning sand around one submerged rock near a pier, I discovered one side of it was literally filled with old bottles yet none were to be found anywhere else at the site.

Following a visual search, metal detecting around wharves can be lucrative in several ways. Often a bottle or piece of china is discovered unintentionally while digging for a metal target. I once found an antique wine bottle attached to a piece of metal conglomerate so it is imperative to keep alert when digging targets. While you may opt to ignore large targets when detecting for jewelry at a swimming beach, it would be an error to ignore them when near a wharf. And this can make detecting a time consuming endeavor since both large and small targets can be in abundance. But keep in mind almost anything imaginable could have been lost beneath a dock including entire purses and nautical hardware such as portholes and ship's gauges.

Due to the amount of trash encountered, some discrimination adjustment is usually necessary when detecting around wharves. If a pier has been standing for many years countless objects have been cast into the water including bottle caps, bait cans and the ever-present fishhooks and fishing weights. If a pier has collapsed from natural causes or burned, chances are the bottom will be littered with nails, screws and bolts. Similar conditions may exist if a pier has been dismantled. There can be some frustration due to the amount of trash encountered however don't be tempted into using more discrimination than required to block out small nails and screws or many valuable targets will be missed.

One method of searching old pier sites incorporates beginning outside the main section and working in toward the more cluttered areas. In this way, the sound of good targets can be ascertained without being overwhelmed by an overabundance of confusing junk targets. By the time you enter the trashy area, the sound of solid targets will be fresh in your mind and make it easier to discern the various sounds. Another

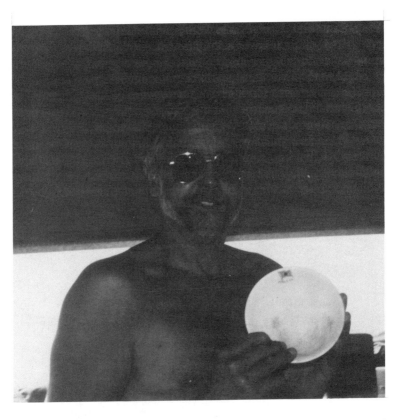

Proper research rewarded the author with this bowl adorned with a steamship company logo.

advantage to this technique is a hot spot may be hit on the outside area of the pier. The search area can then be widened using this spot as a center point.

When working the trashy area of a pier it can sometimes be advantageous to take a break from the junk and venture to the outer perimeter of the search area. There are often good targets to be found away from the wharf and a break from trash can help clear the mind making detecting more enjoyable and productive.

Research is the key to successfully diving the right area of a pier. This is especially true if minimal remains of the original structure are in evidence. Old photographs can be extremely valuable since they can provide line-ups on shore and reveal details regarding the length of the pier, where ships tied-up, and any structures which may have been constructed to house passengers or ticket agents. Some piers even had saloons or stores built atop as an integral part of their purpose.

While treasure hunting around underwater structures can be enjoyable and lucrative for a prepared diver, it can be potentially dangerous to an unprepared novice due to the difficult conditions often encountered. The following guidelines are offered in an effort to add safety to your diving and, just maybe, that special coin or relic to your collection.

A search is always warranted near an older building since many structures located on the waterfront had piers extending into the adjacent water.

Preparation

Diving conditions can vary greatly around submerged structures. Some old docks are located in crystal-clear water with mere stumps for pilings creating no obstacle for the diver. Other structures are in dirty water and have overhangs which can impede an ascent. A general rule, however, is a pier or structure is no place to learn to dive. Advanced certification and experience are generally imperative when searching around most structures.

Limited visibility is the first obstacle to be expected when searching an underwater structure since many docks and piers are found in enclosed bays. Even if the water happens to be reasonably clear when you enter, it probably won't be after you start digging through the sand or mud bottom. While zero visibility can be unnerving at times, the problem can be magnified by a nearby underwater structure.

An example of the potential danger presented by this combination occurred to a treasure hunting companion. Mike is an accomplished diver and veteran treasure hunter. One afternoon, as he searched an area for a possible site to dive, he was intrigued by a group of pilings jutting from the water's surface. Within a few minutes, he was suited-up and entered the brackish liquid to investigate the old dock.

Visibility was minimal--maybe a foot. He followed the bank downward using a light as an aid until he hit the bottom at 30 feet. The bottom search proved relatively unproductive so he cut the dive short and started to surface. However, as he began his ascent he immediately slammed into solid wood. At first, the wood was a mere source of confusion. But as he explored in several directions, and the planks remained above him impairing any escape, panic began to swell from within; he now knew the original pier had collapsed and he had unknowingly penetrated below it. He had no way of knowing how large the pier was or in what direction he should swim to escape entrapment

Mike relied on his experience and suppressed the panic. He methodically began searching for the pier's end or at least an opening. While he could not see the planks, he followed the contour by touch until finally his arm penetrated an opening. But as he felt for the perimeter of the hole it was soon apparent it was not large enough for him to slip through. As precious air hissed toward empty, he had no choice but to remove his tank and BC and try to squeeze through the opening.

Visibility shot to zero as the mud bottom stirred from his movement. Once his BC was removed he felt for the hole and forced his way through then pulled his tank upward and, with elation, made his way to the surface.

This story is not related to terrify the reader. It's told simply because it's true. If Mike hadn't the experience in limited visibility diving, I have little doubt he'd still be trapped below the pier.

A good way to prepare for limited visibility diving is by beginning in a pool. This can be accomplished by installing black cardboard on the inside of your mask. You and your buddy can become acclimated to limited conditions by "feeling" for the location of your pressure gauge, safe second stage, knife, etc. within a safe environment. The experience may also reduce the typical anxiety associated with limited visibility diving.

While practicing in the pool, it is a good time to discuss and practice signals and emergency procedures as well. One of the more difficult challenges in limited visibility diving is communicating and keeping track of one another while underwater.

Equipment

Once you're trained and comfortable with diving in limited visibility, specialized equipment is the next important step. The equipment required for a dive can vary depending on the type of structure, depth, conditions, etc. But it is always a good idea to analyze your needs thoroughly prior to entering the water.

A dive light is probably not necessary in clean or shallow water but sunlight is quickly dispersed at about 20 feet in dirty or muddy water. The depth at which a light is needed is relative to water conditions but it can be assumed a light is required when dropping down in water with less than two or three feet visibility.

A Smith and Wesson revolver, c. 1914, was discovered near an old dock.

One of the more important items required for diving around structures and/or limited visibility diving is a downline which is discussed in detail in Chapter 2. Downlines can be anchored to the bottom then buoyed with a float or in some cases it may be advantageous to run a line down the bank to the bottom. Once while exploring a canal, I found it worked well to have two downlines anchored on either side of the canal with another line stretching across the bottom and attached to each anchor. To search I simply followed the line down then across the channel. I then moved the downline anchors over slightly to search a new area.

A reel, also discussed in Chapter 2, can be a critical tool when searching an area of limited visibility or around structures. The primary advantage of a reel is it leads the way home and you don't have to surface near the structure or in a

Some items discovered around structures can be fairly old and require extreme care when handling such as this water pitcher, c.1850.

Although there is no remaining evidence on the surface, this lake was once a thriving resort with countless docks and piers.

current or in possible boat traffic to find the correct direction. Nor do you have to strain your eyes to see a compass bearing. You just pay out the line while exploring, then wind it up and it leads you back to where you started.

Any time a diver ventures into an enclosed space, appropriate training, such as a recognized cave or wreck diving specialty course, and a reel are a must. While visibility may seem acceptable when entering, it can quickly turn to zero when years of silt are stirred from the bottom. A safety line securely attached to the point of entry and reeled out while exploring is required to provide the direction back for a safe exit. A reel may be attached to the bottom of a downline while diving off docks. In this way, you'll always know the way clear.

While a submersible pressure gauge should always be an integral part of your diving equipment, it is essential when

These remnants of the past were discovered by divers below the surface of a fresh water landing.

Ocean piers from the same era usually yield similar items as evidenced by steamship china, bottles, an insulator and the remains of a brass fishing reel.

diving in difficult conditions. Typically, divers use more air while diving in limited visibility. Also, the physical demands of digging and sand fanning will cause a tank to empty much faster than during a casual dive. For these reasons a pressure gauge should be checked more frequently when diving under adverse conditions.

A knife is required when diving around structures. While entanglement is not necessarily a hazard in most diving conditions, it is a possibility when diving around structures or docks. The usual culprits are fishing line or discarded anchor line which can be in abundance. Lost fishing nets can also be a source of entanglement. But it is not a good idea to rely on a knife to cut your way out of a net. Swaying fishing nets are a formidable adversary and it is much better to abort the dive if

Some discoveries are quite valuable or rare. The diver above displays a 1917-S quarter found in pristine condition.

they're encountered.

A compass is a useful tool to a treasure diver even when using lines or reels. By taking compass bearings prior to submerging, a compass will point the way back, aid in making an effective search pattern and is a useful back-up to a reel. Most underwater compasses have large, luminous markings for easy reading in dark conditions. Use only the type which is designed for underwater applications and has a rotating bezel for navigation.

There are several unique problems incurred in this type of diving which makes independence a necessity. Limited

A Cabinet Kentucky Bourbon bottle, c. 1880, found at a fresh water site has a value of around $700.00.

The diver holds an antique brass case filled with percussion caps.

visibility can make it next to impossible to find your buddy in an emergency. Also, a floating dock or other structure can impair an emergency swimming ascent. For these reasons an independent air source is extremely valuable. The only true independent air source includes both a separate tank and a separate regulator. A safe second stage is not an independent air source.

A technique commonly used in deep diving can also be used in limited visibility diving. A flashing light beacon can be attached to the bottom of your downline. A strobe-type light can be a welcome sight when disoriented in muddy water.

Prior to making your first dive near a structure, it's advisable to "streamline" your equipment. It's relatively easy to get hung-up on underwater objects, especially in limited visibility. This can sometimes be avoided by limiting the external protrusions on your equipment. Pressure gauge hoses should be attached and not allowed to hang freely. A goody bag should be tucked into itself prior to attaching it to your weight belt. The ends of mask straps should be taped. On some types of fins it's possible to reverse the strap so the free ends are on the inside. If this isn't possible, they can be taped with electrical tape. And if using a metal detector, make sure the cord is wound tightly around the shaft as previously described.

Making The Dive

Prior to entering the water, a surface survey should be performed. Make a plan with your buddy regarding entry and exit points, where to place the downline, bottom time, etc. Check each other's equipment for potential problems and take the time to carefully observe the area for boat traffic, fishermen, surf, currents or any other condition which could complicate the dive.

Always ease into the water when diving around submerged objects, especially if you're unfamiliar with the site. A giant stride entry directly atop a submerged pier piling is an experience one should try to avoid.

As mentioned, the first dive on a pier site should be done without a detector since some objects may be in plain view. But there is another value to an underwater survey before serious searching begins. Obstacles such as fishing nets, sharp objects and rusted metal could be everywhere yet the dangers may not be noticed when concentrating on metal detecting.

This latter point is extremely important. I once was diving a wreck that had gone aground along a rugged shoreline. Visibility was about three feet with swells about the same. While concentrating on my search pattern, I didn't notice I had ventured into an area where hundreds of jagged pieces of metal projected from the bottom. A large set of waves suddenly sent me careening through the mass of steel. I narrowly escaped being impaled on one razor-sharp piece of steel by mere inches. It was a foolish mistake, one which I'd suggest avoiding at all cost.

When exiting the water, always use the downline for ascent.

Limited visibility offers few reference points to judge ascent rate. The downline also provides security against ascending against the bottom of a boat hull or structure. When diving around docks or any floating structure, it's also advisable to ascend with one hand or your detector held above your head to prevent an unexpected collision. As always, a dive flag and surface float are a must to warn boaters of your presence.

If properly executed, treasure hunting around structures can be a safe and profitable venture. Thousands of old docks and landings await discovery and, with a little research, one near you may very well conceal that special treasure as well.

This diver discovered two steamship luggage tags in plain sight near an old wharf. One of the tags had never been seen before by experts. (Photo-Western and Eastern Treasures)

Two prized whiskey bottles discovered by a diver at a deep-water landing.

CHAPTER 5.

Treasure In Deep Water

Treasure sites infinitely vary. Some locations seem to welcome the explorer with pleasant weather and benign conditions while others are both foreboding to the treasure hunter and hostile to his equipment. An example of the latter is the deep ocean where treasures abound, yet few people are drawn to search for them.

Many might think in terms of miles when imagining deep treasure hunting. And most certainly the deepest ocean can no longer hide its secrets with recent advances in technology. However, for most treasure hunters 60-130 feet might be a more realistic figure when searching with conventional scuba equipment and breathing air. At about 60 feet, the first serious repercussions of depth begin to affect the diver in both limited no-decompression time and residual nitrogen problems. At around 100 feet, nitrogen narcosis begins to impair the diver's judgment and creates anxiety. As the depth increases, the concerns proportionately magnify in severity until reaching 130 feet which is the maximum safe diving limit on air set by the U.S. Navy.

Because of these and other diving complications, searching for a deep site is best done from the surface. There are ample electronic gadgets manufactured for this purpose. Some are

A fathometer (left) and a G.P.S. unit can be used effectively to find submerged objects in deeper water.

prohibitively expensive for us average folks but in the event you don't happen to have a deep submersible in your garage, there's still hope. Numerous devices are available in which to search deeper water that are economical yet effective.

Fathometers

A fathometer is an inexpensive gauge that reads the water's depth. But in doing so, it also graphs submerged reefs, rocks and anything else that projects upward from the bottom, such as shipwrecks or pilings. Searching the ocean bottom with a fathometer is often called "metering" and, generally speaking, requires three people. One individual is needed to steer the boat on an exact course, one monitors the fathometer and another person stands by to throw a marker buoy over the side when a "bump" is discovered.

The key to successful metering is attention to detail. The course must be maintained as true as possible to eliminate overlapping or missing part of the search area. A Loran system or a G.P.S. unit (Global Positioning System) is almost a necessity to ensure this. G.P.S. units receive signals from orbiting satellites and translate them into position, course, etc., with incredible accuracy. Also, metering requires careful monitoring of the fathometer since older wrecks or obstacles may barely rise above the ocean bottom. While a fathometer is an inexpensive alternative, its use is limited to flat substrates where a rise in the bottom is the exception rather than the rule. Another disadvantage is a fathometer covers a relatively small search area with each pass.

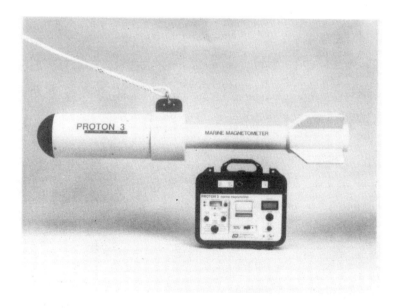

The J.W. Fishers Proton 3 magnetometer. Magnetometers have discovered more shipwreck sites than any other device.

Magnetometers

When exploring a rocky or uneven bottom or searching for shipwrecks, a proton magnetometer may be a better choice. Since inception, magnetometers have discovered more major shipwreck sites than any other device and are the primary choice of most serious underwater treasure hunters.

A magnetometer is a towable "fish" which detects anomalies in the earth's magnetic field caused by ferrous metal. Once an object is detected, the signal is then relayed up to a monitor on the search boat where the location of the "hit" is graphed by the machine or can be plotted or marked by a buoy. A magnetometer works well above most any terrain, however it is of use only with ferrous metal such as anchors, iron cannon or other iron objects and does not detect gold, silver, bronze or other nonferrous metals.

One of the more popular magnetometers is the Proton 3 manufactured by J.W. Fishers. This moderately-priced unit offers a maximum detection range of 1,500 feet for larger objects and is capable of detecting a one gallon can at 12 feet. The Proton 3 is the third generation of magnetometers made by J.W. Fishers and features several available options including Loran/G.P.S. interface capabilities.

Side Scan Sonar

Side scan sonar is another useful tool when searching for wrecks. Although more expensive than most proton magnetometers, a side scan unit does not require a magnetic anomaly and will register most anything as long as it's not completely buried. Side scan sonar works by sending beams laterally across the ocean bottom from both sides of a towable fish. The beams echo off any object projecting from the bottom and are then received by transducers and interpreted into a graphic image on a video screen and/or paper recorder.

The SSS-100K Side Scan Sonar, for example, is also manufactured by J. W. Fishers. It is capable of descending down to 500 feet and detecting small targets at 40 feet and

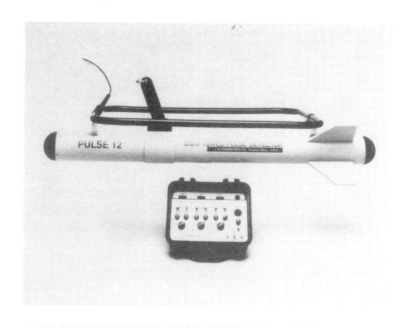

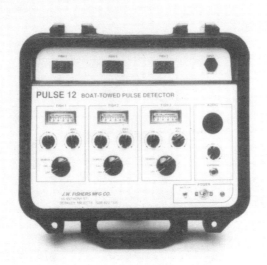

The Pulse 12 boat-towed pulse induction metal detector and control box.

larger objects to 1,800 feet on either side of the fish. The readings are then printed on two, eight inch graphs, one graph for each side. A distinct advantage to side scan sonar is it not only detects an object, it graphs an outline of its appearance.

Boat-Towed Metal Detectors

The boat-towed underwater metal detector is another device which can be used to locate shipwrecks or other metal debris. While it does not have the range of a magnetometer, it can detect any metal and is not limited to ferrous metal exclusively. The Pulse 12 (shown) has a detection range of up to 16 feet deep by 24 feet wide. A one gallon can may be detected within an area approximately six feet deep and nine feet wide. While not as long-range as side scan sonar or magnetometers, up to three fish can be operated from one control box to increase the search area.

Underwater Video Cameras

Another alternative for searching the deep ocean is the video camera. Since a camera doesn't require magnetic metal or any rise in altitude from the bottom, it can be especially useful for searching out old dump sites or deep water piers. Numerous companies manufacture underwater video camera housings and there are specialized underwater search cameras as well. However, before selecting a camera, keep in mind there is extremely low light at depth so a camera must be able to operate in such limited conditions or lights must be added.

There are two types of underwater video cameras used in treasure hunting. One is a towable fish which is generally used for searching. The other is a dropped camera which simply hangs off the search boat to survey the bottom. The latter is especially useful in determining the search boat's position over a site prior to diving. The downside of the underwater video camera is it requires fair water visibility to be effective.

Remotely Operated Vehicles

For those who require more sophisticated equipment, a remotely operated vehicle (ROV) is a definite must. An ROV is literally an extension of the operator and is like diving without getting wet. ROVs can descend much deeper than divers. They can go most any direction at the operator's command and even penetrate a wreck with an experienced "pilot" at the helm. Depending on the type, an ROV can perform numerous tasks while simultaneously sending a visual image back to the operator in the search vessel. And with the aid of a VCR, it can make a permanent record of the site as well.

ROVs have received most of their notoriety on ultra-deep water salvage operations such as those performed on the "Titanic" and "Central America." While an ROV is not exactly an item you'll purchase by saving pocket change, a new generation is now being borne which reflects a realistic price tag for the smalltime salvage firm.

Underwater Altimeters

With any towable electronic device, an underwater altimeter is an important option. An altimeter lets the operator know the depth between the "fish" and the bottom. Some are also equipped with an adjustable alarm in the event of sudden depth changes. While an underwater altimeter does not find treasure, it may very well save from loss your equipment that does.

Once a site has been discovered, the next step is to investigate it personally. This requires specialized training as well as equipment. But it is an experience one doesn't soon forget.

A drop-type video camera can be lowered to identify underwater sites (opposite page), or can be mounted in a protective cage with a stabilizing wing for towed searches.

83.

Exploring The Deep

Few experiences compare with diving into a sea of seemingly endless depth. Just such a dive was described in an article I wrote for "*Western and Eastern Treasures*" magazine:

"The anchor line angled downward then faded from sight into inky darkness. I allowed air to hiss from my buoyancy compensator then slowly began my descent down the taut rope. Although awkwardness had disappeared, I could still feel resistance from the twin tanks and pony bottle strapped to my back as the current swept by at an uncomfortable four knots. At 25 feet, the surface dimmed from view and all reference points were now abandoned save the white anchor line and ever-moving needle on my depth gauge.

"My free-fall speed noticeably increased due to the compression of my wetsuit as I zipped passed the 50 foot mark. I vented air into my BC and buoyancy returned to only slightly negative. Color had now all but disappeared into a washed-out green haze as I continued my downward plunge.

"At 75 feet, I entered a surrealistic transition where a deep-ocean upwelling melded with warmer surface water. The temperature dropped abruptly as I entered the thermocline, but that was not the most dramatic change; I descended into an eerie layer where the liquids seemingly refused to merge. The resultant vision appeared somewhat out of focus, transparent yet alive with movement. The sensation ended as quickly as it had begun as I slipped ever downward. I glanced at my depth gauge. The needle pointed to 100 feet yet the anchor line continued downward with no apparent end.

"Suddenly, time lost meaning. It seemed an hour had passed since I last checked my watch and depth gauge. I lifted my wrist and console to my mask which revealed less than a minute had, in reality, elapsed. Nitrogen narcosis, I thought to myself. I had expected the phenomenon but was caught off-guard by its dramatic affect.

"A massive shadow suddenly loomed from the distance. It had no detail or identifiable characteristics, only a colorless image against dark nothingness. I continued my descent. With each passing foot, details began to appear. First, ribs with attached knees, then a fishnet swaying in the invisible current, then planks adorned with greenish brass spikes. With nervous anticipation I left the security of the downline and swam down to the spectacular sight to make the most of the mere ten minutes my dive plan allowed."

Such was one of my early deep-diving experiences. I can think of only a few reasons for descending beyond the depths of normal recreational diving. For most deep divers, it is the lure of sunken ships or other treasures which have somehow transcended the world of air and light and made their way down to a far ocean bottom. But while these treasures may be alluring, searching the deep has its share of risks and challenges which require careful and methodical consideration. And knowledge of proper search techniques is essential for success.

Deep-diving is not an endeavor to be considered by novices and advanced training is mandatory. A rule of thumb is beginning divers should stay above 60 feet and experienced divers without specialized training should not exceed 100 feet. The reasons for this are numerous. First, there is nitrogen narcosis with which deep-divers must contend. At about 100 feet the increased partial pressure on the nitrogen in air creates a narcotic effect. This affects different people to varying degrees and the symptoms are not always consistent. There is also the limited no-decompression time allowed at depth. At 130 feet, a diver has only 10 minutes (U.S. Navy Tables) from beginning of descent to beginning of ascent. This is not much time and a dive must be planned and executed perfectly to achieve optimum results. There is also the concern with a limited air supply. At deeper depths a tank lasts a fraction of what can be expected in shallow water.

If that's not enough, there are numerous other repercussions noticed while descending into deep water. Wetsuits compress leaving once-tight straps loose and sagging. Warmth disappears and cold numbs both the body and mind. Every diving concern--breathing resistance, blocks, squeezes, loss of buoyancy--become magnified.

Because of the intricacies involved, safety measures become imperative while deep-diving. A downline is an absolute must when descending or ascending from a deep site since visual contact with both the surface and the bottom is usually lost.

Some deep-water search equipment can be made by the average diver. This homemade underwater video camera and fish utilizes a small surveillance camera mounted in a still camera housing.

Another reason for utilizing a downline is unseen currents can sweep a diver off course since reference points are nonexistent.

Once at the bottom, another line should be attached to the downline to mark a path back for ascent. Do not trust a compass bearing to find a thin line in the middle of the ocean. Here again, the diving reel is an imperative piece of equipment.

Often, the initial target has been missed by the marker buoy and an underwater search is required. The easiest search method is with a dropped video camera. But if diving is necessary, an accurate search may be achieved by swimming in a circular pattern around the anchor while paying out line from a reel. The amount of line to release on each pass is relative to visibility and conditions.

As always, a competent dive buddy is all-important and both divers should know proper hand signals and emergency procedures. Divers should spend ample time together in shallow water learning to work as a team prior to descending into the deep. Since an emergency swimming ascent is unlikely at depth, you are literally trusting your life to your dive buddy and should feel comfortable doing so.

Prior to a deep-dive, both divers should be well rested and in good mental and physical condition. A good meal is important 2-3 hours prior to the dive and no alcohol should be consumed 24 hour before diving. It is also important to verify the location of the nearest recompression chamber before venturing into the deep.

Discuss the dive plan before entering the water and execute it religiously regardless of what you find. No treasure is worth the bends. Also, it is important both divers wear an independent air source which contains enough air for a safe return to the downline and a proper ascent. A decompression meter should also be worn in addition to appropriate and conservative pre-dive planning with decompression tables. And never push the tables. I have known several divers who were within their no-decompression limits yet found themselves in a recompression chamber.

When deep-diving, it is imperative each diver logs the time when beginning descent and writes it on a slate. The depth should additionally be logged on the slate immediately upon reaching the bottom, then the time again logged when ending

Diving deep-water sites can be challenging but the rewards can be worth the effort. These vintage bottles were discovered in 100 feet of water in an old port.

the dive and beginning ascent. While a computer may be logging the times for you, it is my belief it should be duplicated just in case of computer failure.

Extra attention must be given to ascent and descent speed keeping in mind descent is not to exceed 75 feet per minute and ascent not to exceed 60 feet per minute.

When first settling on a deep ocean bottom, keep leg movement to a minimum since fins can kick up silt and cloud visibility, and check your weight belt buckle to make sure wetsuit compression hasn't shifted it to the back or side. And always remember to make a decompression stop at 15 feet for three minutes even though you're within no-decompression limits.

A diver makes a decompression stop using the anchor line for reference. A stop at 15 feet for three minutes is an important safety factor even if a diver is within no-decompression limits.

Altitude Conversion

While the techniques for hunting deep salt and fresh water are about the same, there is a factor which should be considered prior to venturing into mountain lakes. Altitude has a dramatic effect on diving due to what is called the "rate of change of pressure." At sea level atmospheric pressure is about 14.7 P.S.I. But if one were to plan a trip to a lake located at an altitude of 10,000 feet, the atmospheric pressure would change to about 10 P.S.I. This difference seems relatively insignificant until we compare the ratio of the change in pressure when ascending from depth.

For example: we know that a diver at sea level adds an additional atmosphere of pressure per every 33 feet of depth so a 66 foot dive adds about 29.4 P.S.I. to the existing atmospheric pressure of 14.7 P.S.I. for total of about 44 P.S.I. At 10,000 feet of altitude, however, the atmospheric pressure is only about 10 P.S.I., so a dive to 66 feet would have an ambient pressure of about 40 P.S.I. These figures seem insignificant until the ratio of the pressure differences is compared. The difference between the change in pressure when surfacing from the altitude dive is four times. That's the approximate equivalent of a dive to over 100 feet at sea level. Hence, several problems.

The first problem is in ascent rate. A normal ascent rate (at one foot per second) from a 66 foot dive at sea level would be 66 seconds. But when making the same dive at an altitude of 10,000 feet, this would be too fast considering the 66 foot depth is the equivalent of about 100 feet. In other words, the ascent from 66 feet of depth when diving at an altitude of 10,000 feet should be around 100 seconds.

There are several simple formulas for altitude conversion. The rule of thumb used to adjust depth at altitude is called the "Four Percent Rule." In essence, 4% of the depth is added to the depth for every 1,000 feet of altitude. For example, if we were planning a dive at a 4,000 foot elevation to a depth of 50 feet, we'd use the formula:

$$4(.04 \times 50) + 50 = 58$$

By using this formula we'd know that our 50 foot dive at an elevation of 4,000 feet is the equivalent of a 58 foot dive at sea level.

There is another rule of thumb formula which can utilized to figure adjusted ascent rates at elevation: simply subtract two feet per minute for each 1,000 feet of altitude. For example, to figure our rate of ascent when diving at 4,000 feet elevation:

$$4 \times 2 = 8 \text{ feet per minute slower ascent}$$
$$60 \text{ feet per minute} - 8 = 52 \text{ feet per minute}$$

There are also problems with depth gauges reading incorrectly when diving at altitude. A capillary tube depth gauge measures the ratio between water pressure to the surface air pressure so can be used for the approximate equivalent depth at altitude. Conversion tables are also available and some dive computers adjust for altitude as well.

Before planning a dive in a mountain lake it is also prudent to consider there's less oxygen in the air. This can be a major factor if a long surface swim is required.

Obviously, a book could be written on deep treasure hunting techniques and this is merely an overview. While searching the deep is not for everyone, proper education and equipment can unveil a world where light barely penetrates, few explore, and countless treasures await.

CHAPTER 6.

Rivers

Steve, Mike and I stood on the rock levee above the brackish river. They were locked in a conversation regarding the dive plan while I scanned the levee for a relatively smooth path down to the water's edge. Mike, with his head still turned away from the river and discussing the dive, suddenly stepped off the road and plowed his way downward through the brush-covered rocks.

"So this is river diving," I mumbled to myself.

As Steve followed Mike's lead I resigned myself to pathlessness and took the mighty step off the road and half-hiked, half-tumbled my way to the river's edge. As I made a perfect though unintentional giant stride into the water, Steve's voice reverberated, "Now you've got it!"

I smiled, sort of, then double-checked the compass bearings written on my slate and let the air hiss from my BC to begin descent. My first observation was visibility was limited to two feet which, according to my comrades, was exceptionally good.

I followed the contour of the levee downward and turned on my light at about 15 feet. At 20 feet, the light became a necessity as the millions of particles suspended above absorbed and reflected most of the sun's rays.

The bottom suddenly leveled out at 25 feet and immediately my eyes caught a glimpse of the reason we were diving here; bottles and pots blanketed the mud. I picked up a few and a mud cloud bellowed upward reducing visibility to zero. I checked my compass but to no avail; I could see nothing. I swam a few feet, checked it again and continued outward from the bank. I was looking for a deeper channel not a mud bank.

Suddenly the bottom disappeared. How does one lose the bottom, I thought. Had I inadvertently ascended? I backtracked a little and discovered a vertical mud wall disappearing into the depths. I had been warned about these walls. They can be firm or dangerously soft and it is imperative to check before following them down. I ran my hand along the edge then into the wall. It was penetrable yet seemed firm enough. I freefell along the wall and into the blackness until at 40 feet I hit the river's bottom.

I sat motionless for just a minute allowing the mud to clear from my landing when suddenly a massive, shadowy skeleton loomed before my eyes. Instinctively, my body retreated until my brain finally recognized a pine tree and not a dead Goliath. Is this fun or what?

I moved slightly away from the tree and mud cliff and scanned the light's eerie beam before me. They were everywhere! Bottles thrown overboard from a landing which had been abandoned over 100 years ago. I was literally surrounded by history, items left untouched until my visit. All apprehension faded as I began systematically inspecting each relic.

Such is a description of one of my early river dives. River diving is like no other. Rivers can be muddy and swift and downright ugly, yet they have a magical attraction. Rivers facilitated some of the earliest forms of transportation in many

It is usually easier to beach a boat and begin a river dive from the shoreline where the current is usually more benign.

This beer bottle was discovered in plain view above a river bottom.

areas and continue to do so today. They are the places of rope swings, Tom Sawyer, riverboats and rafts, of heroes and villains and Indians. Just about anything the imagination can dream has happened on a river.

While rivers are a prime target for treasure hunting, they are also a formidable adversary. One of the first challenges in river diving is choosing the correct time to dive. On many rivers the current is simply too swift to dive during certain seasons or hours of the day. Generally, the summer and fall are the best seasons to dive rivers since winter is usually too cold and spring brings run-off and swift water from melting snow. The best time to dive, however, can depend on additional

The bottom of many river landings are littered with debris including numerous types of bottles.

factors. In agricultural regions, heavy harvesting can cloud the water with debris. Irrigation can also affect visibility in much the same way in addition to the danger of intake pipes suctioning river water for adjacent fields. Ocean tides can affect a river dramatically by increasing or reversing the current. Some rivers become so congested with summer boat traffic that diving would indeed be a dangerous endeavor. While there are no certain rules that apply to every river, it is imperative to do a little research before descending.

Pre-dive preparation is just as important as research in river diving. Current speed is the first factor which must be determined when preparing to dive a river. Generally, most

River landings and dumps can sometimes be found in front of old houses and structures which still stand.

divers can contend with a two or three knot current. This is not necessarily easy mind you, but it can be done. The simplest way to determine the current speed is to wait on the bank until something floats by. If the object lazily meanders downstream, it's safe to dive. If it zips by faster than you can identify it, go find another site.

In most rivers, the current is fastest on the outside edge of a turn and slows on the inside. And there is a paradox in this. The inside bank may be the most benign conditions for diving yet may be silted in or completely filled with a sand bar due to the slow current speed.

While it may be tempting to forge ahead despite a swift current, diving in a fast current is usually an unproductive

Some sites require research and a keen eye to locate. These overgrown steps are all that remain of a once-vital river port.

endeavor at best. There was one site I was determined to explore in which the current flushed through at about 10 knots, and the center of channel where the current was the fastest was the exact area I wanted to search. I figured if I beached my boat, threw the anchor into the channel and tied the other end off at the bank, I could simply follow the line down. The dive started out all right, but then I hit the swiftest part of the current. I suddenly became like a flag in a wind storm. I was so busy trying to hang onto the anchor line there wasn't much hope of looking for anything. It was a site I quickly abandoned for better conditions.

Some individuals have tried drift dives in rivers utilizing a chase boat. This might work in a reasonably slow current, but I wouldn't suggest it in any current which you can't swim against. First, there's not much chance of locating anything in limited visibility when you fly by at the speed of light. Also, there's a fair possibility the current might sweep you below a log or other obstruction and keep you pinned in place. Thirdly, I just don't know anyone I personally would trust enough to drive the chase boat.

Once a suitable site has been located, compass bearings must be taken prior to entering the water. I personally find it best to draw a diagram on my slate and list the directions up river and to the side I plan on exiting. While it may seem unnecessary to have both bearings, keep in mind the current does not always tell you the direction down river. Eddies can reverse the current making life confusing to say the least.

After taking the proper bearings, an entry site must be determined if diving from the shoreline. There is only one problem here; I have found there are very few good entry points on most rivers. Usually the banks are steep, uneven and loaded with brush. But it never hurts to give it a proper search anyway.

Entering the water must be done slow and easy, no huge leaps or you might find yourself down river a couple of miles. Keep low and close to the ground when approaching the water, then keep on the bottom following its contour the entire descent. It should go without saying that you should always swim up-current when exploring a river, then you can just ride it back to your exit point at the end of the dive.

It can be assumed that most river dives will be similar to night dives since it usually becomes quite dark at about 20 feet of depth. This in itself, is not so bad except for the fact that obstacles are commonplace. On one outing, my companions and I discovered two cars and a van, one of which had been used in a robbery, in addition to almost every type of appliance imaginable. Rivers, it seems, are universal dumping grounds, and it is for this reason they make for interesting explorations. But they are also filled with hazards such as monofilament line, abandoned fishing nets, trees and stumps and all kinds of nasty things you don't want to run into.

There is not much hope of avoiding all obstacles while diving in a river, but there are several ways to minimize the

River bottoms can be covered with old and unusual items, some of which are valued by collectors.

Research is the key to discovering sites which have no visible pilings or nearby structures. Although there was nothing to indicate a once-thriving port, numerous items were discovered on the bottom of this site.

danger. First, dive when the current is minimal and stay close to the bottom. The river bottom usually causes drag on the current and tends to slow it down a bit. Rocks on the bottom can also provide handholds which can help in preventing an unexpected down river voyage. Another way to avoid obstacles is to go slow. Allow time to scan your light in front, above and to the sides before you move forward. Going slow may help in avoiding an unwanted obstacle and it's a good treasure hunting habit to adopt anyway.

Perhaps the most frightening aspect of river diving is the

Steamship china is one of the more sought after prizes in river diving.

possibility of entrapment. And it is totally possible to venture into an enclosed space without even knowing it in such limited visibility. For this reason, it is advisable to dive with someone familiar with the site, at least on the first few dives. A diving reel is also a handy tool to lead your way back to safety.

With all this to consider one might well ask, why dive a river? There are three primary answers: swimming holes, landings and old dumps. Most rivers have lagoons or sloughs where the water tends to slow or stop. These inlets are usually popular swimming areas for contemporary bathers and may have been in use for many years. Like any beach, a river swimming hole may very well contain both coins and jewelry.

The unique challenge in diving river swimming holes is finding a suitable bottom. Many areas of slow current tend to fill with silt making detecting almost useless. A simple test can be performed in this case to see if further exploration is warranted. Many divers simply plunge their hand into the muck. If your arm penetrates deeper than the elbow, the site will probably not give up any of its secrets. If the mud is a thin layer above rocks or gravel, it may very well be a lucrative site to hunt, although some trenching of the mud may be necessary. One little hint: when testing the mud's depth a stick or probe is safer than a hand. If you insist on using an appendage, make a fist before plunging your hand into the bottom since a lost wetsuit glove may otherwise result, and watch for glass, rusty metal and any other ugly that could alter the state of your skin.

Old dumps are another interesting target to explore. Unlike swimming beaches, dumps contain articles intentionally discarded rather than lost inadvertently, which can be a distinct advantage to a treasure hunter. Usually, these dumps will be located in the main channel of a river although sloughs and other inlets may have also been dumping grounds in the past. For obvious reasons, only old dumps are worth searching since they may contain bottles, pots and almost anything else that once lost its value but now is an antique.

There are several ways to locate an old river dump. Generally, if there is an antiquated house along the river, there is a dump directly in front. The early residents of the home had to do something with their trash and you can almost be assured it ended up in the river.

Old maps are another way to locate old dumping sites although they probably will not be listed so obviously as "old dump." Maps of yesteryear provide locations of settlements long since abandoned such as canneries, forts, mills, ferry crossings and lumber landings. Sometimes, a settlement may consist of only a farm or a few houses, but still, odds are a dump is directly in front.

Another way to locate dumps is by searching for a land protrusion on a river. This is often only a mere "bump" of land protruding into the water. Normally, a road ends at this tiny peninsula so people could simply back their wagons, trucks and cars up to the river and dump the garbage.

Searching for dumps should not be done exclusively since old landings may be discovered simultaneously. Just about all settlements and towns had at least one landing. In agricultural

One group of lucky divers stumbled onto a river dump near a Chinese settlement abandoned since the late 1800s. The numerous finds included white "eggshell" bottles, tiger whiskey jugs, soy sauce jugs, saki bottles and a variety of other containers.

areas, most farms had a landing to facilitate loading their crops for market. Many times pilings or stumps of pilings from old landings can still be seen breaking the surface of the water so research can be limited to driving up and down a levee road or cruising the river with a boat. Old maps can also be an invaluable source of information.

Like dumps, landings usually provide an infinite variety of items scattered across the river bottom. Discarded bottles are among the most common discoveries, but it's possible to uncover objects like rifles, pistols, fire extinguishers, steamship china and luggage. You name it and it may have been dropped or thrown off the wharf or a visiting riverboat.

Stumps of pilings projecting from the water's surface always indicate a landing or port.

There are a couple of tricks to successfully diving a dump or landing in a main river channel. There are usually three types of bottoms encountered: mud, rock and sand/gravel. When first entering the water, mud is commonly encountered. But this is not the best area to search. A channel etched into the bottom by the current may exist farther from the bank and in deeper water. Bottle hunters refer to this area as the "bottle channel." In these channels, the mud has been swept away and replaced by sand and gravel, and lying above the sand may be a myriad of goodies.

If rock is encountered in deeper water, it usually means the current is or has been strong and has swept away the sand and gravel, and possibly the bottles along with it. But this may or may not be the case. It's a strange phenomenon but I've seen high water surge through an area at incredible speed, yet subsequent dives proved everything was swept away except for the bottles. But any time a rock bottom is encountered a careful search is mandated. Often when the bottom has been swept clean by swift water, metal, coins and heavier objects can be found in the exposed cracks and crevices.

If a mud bottom continues and no other channel can be located, it probably means little will be found and it's best to try the other side of the river (after testing the mud's thickness, of course).

While river diving can be rewarding and lucrative, it is not to be taken lightly. A diver must be extremely skilled before attempting river diving and advanced or higher certification is required. It is, indeed, one of the more difficult environments to penetrate.

CHAPTER 7.

Underwater Salvage

It's just a matter of time before an underwater treasure hunter locates an item that is simply too large to safely transport to the surface without help. Some of the items encountered which require lifting devices are outboard motors, anchors, tool boxes or a collection of bottles.

The common temptation when such an item is encountered is to grab hold of the object and use your buoyancy compensator for lifting. This is the big NO NO! Using a buoyancy compensator for lifting purposes is extremely dangerous. While it's true most BCs have enough buoyancy to bring many items to the surface, an uncontrolled ascent is the result if it is dropped. Even if a BC is vented during the uncontrolled ascent, it has been filled substantially over the diver's neutral buoyancy and will continue to inflate due to the decreasing pressure of the ascent, hence an embolism or other malady is almost assured.

There are numerous lifting devices which make raising an object to the surface both easy and safe. The simplest method is attaching a line to the item and hoisting it to the surface. For multiple smaller objects such as bottles, the line can be tied to a basket or bucket drill with holes which can be filled on the bottom then brought to the surface.

When diving from a boat, an item can be attached to the anchor chain and hoisted simultaneously with the anchor. But this technique is usually reserved for small objects and boats with anchor winches, and keep in mind the bow is the bumpiest place on earth. Wrestling with the line, chain, anchor and retrieved object while balancing on the bow is certainly a challenge.

While these methods work in many situations, they're strictly limited to lighter objects. For larger objects a buoyant device is a must. To fully understand lift bags and other buoyant lifting devices, a review of some basic physics is required.

Archimedes principle states that any object will float if it displaces an amount of water equal to or greater than its own weight. Since salt water weighs 64 pounds per cubic foot, an item weighing 64 pounds would require displacement of one cubic foot or more to float. The same concept is true in fresh water with the exception fresh water weighs 62.4 pounds per cubic foot yet requires more buoyancy for lifting due to the lack of salt. Keep in mind, an item must displace an equal amount of water to its own weight. Therefore a lead ball will not float due to its density, however the same amount of lead will float if redesigned into a configuration that displaces its own weight.

Lift Bags

Utilizing a lift bag to bring an item to the surface is one of the safest and most effective ways to displace an object's weight. A lift bag is merely an inverted bag, open at the bottom with an attached harness. The bag is usually constructed from neoprene, strong canvas or other suitable material. The harness is generally made from wide strips of nylon webbing which are sewn over the top of the bag leaving enough length at the bottom to attach the object which requires lifting. Often a brass shackle or clip is sewn onto the bottom of the harness to make attaching the bag both simple and secure.

Lift bags are rated by pounds of lift. For most small items, a 50, 75 or 100 pound bag will do the job. But lift bags are available to hoist almost anything of any weight.

Lift bags have a distinct advantage over other lifting devices

Anchors are but one of the many items which require a lifting device to safely bring to the surface.

109.

in that they take up minimal space when not in use. A smaller bag can easily be carried rolled in a diver's goody bag just in case a larger object is encountered. Larger bags can be stored in a rather compact area on most small boats.

Using a lift bag is relatively simple but a few rules should be followed. A lift bag is designed for a controlled ascent. In other words, the idea is not to fill the bag and let it go. For this reason, once the bag is properly secured to an object, it should be filled slowly and with just enough air to move the object off the bottom. This can be accomplished several ways. On smaller lift bags, a diver can slip the exhaust port of his regulator under the bag opening while breathing normally. In this way the bag fills slowly without using excess air from the diver's supply. A safe second stage can also be utilized by pushing the purge button while holding it under the bag. On larger items, a separate tank or a surface supplied hose can be used.

In this latter scenario, a simple mechanism can be created for filling any lifting device from a separate air supply. Attach a low pressure, second stage hose to a regulator first stage low pressure port, then attach a standard shop-type air nozzle with a trigger where the second stage would ordinarily be installed. The trigger makes it easy to control the amount of air filling the bag and by using a separate air source no air is taken away from the diver's supply.

Often the weight of the object accounts for only part of the resistance to movement since mud or sand can create a suction of sorts. For this reason, it is a good idea to try to roll or shake the object periodically while filling the bag. If an object is seriously buried with only a small part protruding, the sand or sediment should be removed prior to attempting to lift it. A dredge or water jet can be used for this purpose. Or if you're like most of us, break out the old ping pong paddle.

Once an item has begun lifting from the bottom, the diver should try to swim alongside and guide it upward. This is not imperative but swimming alongside the lift bag can ensure it doesn't get swept away by unseen currents or rise directly under a boat hull. But never guide a lift bag from below and make sure no one is diving beneath just in case the object falls from the harness. And never allow a rising lift bag to dictate a rapid ascent rate. If it is rising faster than your smallest bubble, let it go.

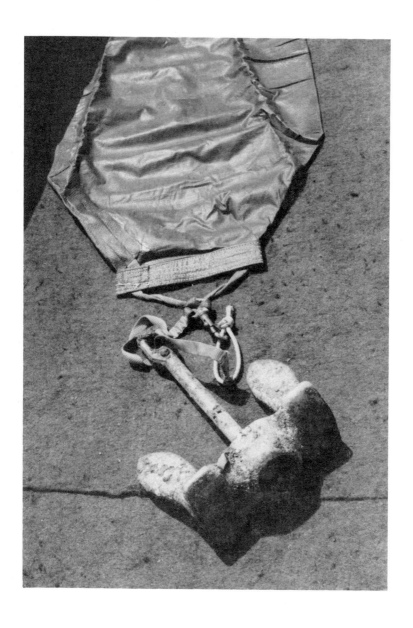

Lift bags come equipped with straps and hardware to securely attach most objects.

It's important to avoid using a lift bag that is larger than required. For example: Let's say you're lifting a small outboard motor from the bottom. A 75 pound lift bag would probably do the job and would simply vent expanding air as it rose to the surface. But let's say you're the ambitious type, after all, if a 75 pound lift bag does the job, a 200 pound bag would do it even better. Right?

Wrong! A 200 pound lift bag would not vent the excess air from the bottom as it ascended; the expanding air would continue to fill the bag causing it to rise faster. This compels the diver to ascend too rapidly to keep up or let go the bag. This scenario is easily avoided by choosing the proper lift bag for each project.

Drums And Barrels

Oil drums are another common tool used for lifting. Most drums hold approximately 45-55 gallons and are capable of lifting approximately 450 pounds. While the ridges used for rolling the barrels work well for attaching lifting slings, there are several problems which must be considered before using barrels on a salvage project.

The first obstacle is their size. Where a lift bag can be rolled and stored, barrels take up a lot of space on a small boat. Another problem is a barrel tends to plummet to the bottom once it is filled with water. Because of this, it can be a tricky maneuver for a diver to ensure the barrel ends up close to the object he wants to lift. For this reason it's best to fill a barrel with just enough water to cause it to sink to avoid a rapid descent.

Because of the lift capacity barrels provide they can be a useful alternative in major salvage work. But this same lifting capacity can cause major problems in controlling the ascent, and untold damage if it happens rise below the salvage boat's hull. For these reasons, it would seem barrels are best left to professional salvors.

Carrying a small lift bag on all dives can be of benefit since most anything can be found when treasure hunting.

Inner Tubes

A regular-sized automobile inner tube may also be used for lifting an object from the bottom. A standard inner tube will lift approximately 100 pounds and two or more can be strapped together for heavier objects. One thing to keep in mind when using an inner tube, or any sealed device, is the air within is going to expand upon ascent, and there is no vent for it to escape. Therefore, the valve cap and core of the inner tube must be removed prior to using it as a lifting device.

Tidal Floats

Sometimes a diver will locate a partially buried item which simply defies lifting due to the suction of the bottom. As mentioned previously, clearing the sand or mud from around the object is the first course of action. However, if the item still refuses to budge, a tidal float might be the answer.

A tidal float is implemented by attaching a line to the sunken object and tying the other end to a barrel or other floating device at the surface during low water. The line should be taught and the floating device of ample buoyancy. The idea is simple. As the tide raises the water level, the floating device will also raise and, theoretically, lift the item which it is attached at the bottom.

Tidal floats can work well in specific situations but have some limitations. First, the object is merely lifted from the bottom not to the surface so a diver will have to ultimately attach another lifting device to the object unless it can be winched to the surface. Another disadvantage is the time frame in which tidal floats work. They usually take several hours to actually lift the object, therefore cannot be used in areas with any boat traffic.

Rigging

Regardless of the buoyancy device utilized, adequate

rigging is essential. When lifting an awkward object, it is more effective to use pre-made slings with shackles or similar hardware rather than rigging knots on the bottom. The reasons for this are twofold; secure knots are difficult to tie underwater and precious air is needlessly wasted on a project that is better done at the surface. Slings can easily be prefabricated in various lengths by attaching a shackle at one end and tying a loop on the other. The sling can then be wrapped around an object several times then the shackle slipped through the loop making a noose which tightens as it is lifted.

If raising an object of substantial weight or size, a salvage manual should be consulted to ensure you're using line, knots and shackles with sufficient strength. Some manuals also detail the approximate weight of various objects, along with useful mathematical formulas. However, unless you have specialized training in such an endeavor, it's best to leave the heavier objects to professionals.

CHAPTER 8.

Excavation

It was my second dive metal detecting the site. The first dive produced numerous newer coins and even a few pieces of jewelry but nothing older than 15 years. This was a mystery considering the beach had been in use for over 100 years. As I settled onto the bottom I decided to fan a small trench just to see what might lay below the layer of soft sand. At about eight inches deep, a layer of compacted rock was encountered. I ran my search coil over the rock and was immediately rewarded with numerous "hits."

The first few targets were nails from a structure which had been destroyed 50 years previously, a good sign I was inching my way toward the past. I loosened the rocks and dug even deeper with more targets registering below the coil. As the trench reached about a foot and a half deep, they finally began to emerge--old coins and relics which had somehow worked their way down through the sand and rock a full two feet.

Deep layers of sand and mud can cover older finds and are the greatest enemies of the underwater treasure hunter. Even newer articles, such as gold rings and chains, can quickly bury themselves due to their high specific gravity. It is indeed a frustrating experience to know treasure is buried at a site, yet too deep to register below a metal detector.

A four inch submersible dredge is relatively easy to handle in the water.

The simplest form of excavation is fanning the sand with your hand or a ping pong paddle, but the depth which can be achieved is extremely limited. However, many of the same techniques utilized in shipwreck salvage can be used on a smaller scale to remove sand and debris effectively and economically.

Dredges

For all intents and purposes dredges are simply underwater vacuum cleaners. A dredge consists of a water pump driven by a gasoline engine which sends water at high velocity down a small hose to a nozzle of larger diameter. The subsequent venturi effect created enables the nozzle to vacuum the bottom. The amount of sand a dredge can remove is based on hose diameter, pump capacity and engine horsepower.

Usually dredges are buoyed by pontoons or inner tubes, or installed in a steel frame for boat use, and are both compact and self-contained. Some are even equipped with an air compressor for surface-supplied diving although some horsepower is diverted from the water pump when this is done.

Dredges come in two types, surface and submersible. Most often the same engine and pump assembly can operate either style. A surface dredge removes the bottom sediment and transports it to the surface where it can be sorted or at least dumped away from the diver. A submersible dredge removes the sediment and merely transports it behind the diver, usually about three or four feet away. Many divers opt to attach extra hose to a submersible dredge nozzle to pipe sediment 10-15 feet in back of the diver. The advantage of the submersible type is much more sand can be moved with less horsepower since the sediment doesn't have to be pumped to the surface.

The type of dredge needed is relative to the expected targets in a specific area. For bottles, steamship china or larger targets that can be seen once they're uncovered, a submersible dredge is probably the best choice since the only objective is to remove the sand to uncover the target. For smaller treasures, a surface dredge is a better choice since the sediment can be directed to a specific sifting area.

A relatively new option for treasure hunters is the coin dredge. In essence, the coin dredge is merely a surface gold dredge with the exception the sluice box and riffle bars have been replaced by a basket. The concept is simple; the surface dredge sucks the sand up to the basket which traps solid objects while the sand and water flow through.

Coin dredges work especially well in sandy or muddy bottoms. However, if rocks or shells are in abundance they will quickly fill the basket rendering it useless. In this case, two people are required to operate it efficiently, one to operate the dredge nozzle and the other to continually sift through and clean the basket.

Operating a dredge is not a particularly difficult task

A submersible dredge pump and engine assembly can be mounted in a small area on a boat.

however a few guidelines should be followed for optimum results. In most cases it is better to focus on uncovering objects rather than sucking them into the intake nozzle. By indiscriminately placing the nozzle in the sand, large rocks and debris will almost certainly be sucked into the hose and cause a jam. Also, fragile objects may break as they're drawn into the metal nozzle. This is easy to avoid by placing the nozzle near the bottom at a slight angle allowing some space between the nozzle and bottom so objects can be seen and larger rocks can be removed before they're extricated. I have found that bending two fingers over the intake hole, thereby reducing its area, also helps stop large rocks from entering the hose.

When hunting a swimming beach for coins and jewelry, a small 2" dredge will do the job. It's true a dredge with a larger diameter hose has more capacity, but the dredge itself is

Many fine objects await discovery entombed below silt and sand bottoms. Buried items are often found in much better condition than those exposed to currents and surge.

considerably more bulky and requires more setup time. Remember, you have to hike this thing to the beach.

For those remote swimming holes, a backpack dredge is a handy device. These are usually limited to a small diameter nozzle, maybe 1", but are extremely compact and easy to assemble.

A submersible dredge can be a larger diameter, however, and still be easy to use. Usually a four to eight inch nozzle is used for excavation yet is still not too cumbersome.

It is difficult to generalize the engine horsepower, pump size and hose diameter combinations for dredges since a lot depends on the depth in which it is being used, whether or not a compressor is installed, etc. Some suggestions are listed.

DREDGE REQUIREMENTS

Suction Hose Diameter	Pressure Inlet	Min. Pump Output
2"	1"	55gpm
3"	1"	100gpm
4"	1 1/2"	125gpm
6"	1 1/2"	300gpm
8"	3"	500gpm

Water Jets

Often the same dredge unit can also provide a reverse action called a water jet. This is accomplished by detaching and using the pressure hose only. The idea is no different than turning on a common garden hose with the exception the pump and gas engine make it portable. Water jets literally blow the sand away. In doing so, visibility is usually reduced to zero which often makes locating objects a bit difficult until the "dust" clears. But they can remove a massive amount of sand in a relatively short time.

A problem not addressed in many water jets is the fact they are like trying to hold onto a jet engine while underwater. This can be exciting, but not profitable. Commercial units provide openings for opposite thrust so the jet is "neutral." These nozzles may be obtained through commercial diving supplies, but are a bit expensive.

Air Lifts

An air lift is a common tool used in shipwreck salvage. It works by pumping air to the lower end of a pipe. As the air flows upward, the bubbles expand due to decreased pressure, hence, suction develops.

An air lift is used in much the same manner as a surface dredge. The items are sucked into the bottom of the pipe and deposited at the other end at the surface. While this works

magnificently, there is a downside for the smalltime salvor. The pipe is rigid and takes up a great deal of space, and it doesn't work well in water less than 20 feet deep. It is also awkward underwater and needs to be rigged and anchored semi-permanently. In other words, it's definitely an overkill for finding a few coins at a swimming beach.

Prop Washes

Mel Fisher of *Atocha* fame is credited with the invention of the prop wash or "mail box." In essence, a prop wash utilizes the dive boat's own propeller(s) for thrust. The thrust is redirected downward by using hollow "elbows" over the props. The current created by this downward thrust can literally blow craters into the sand, uncovering any objects within.

An advantage to prop washes is they blow clean surface water downward to the bottom. While a substantial current can be created, a diver can effectively search the area with good visibility at the same time the prop wash is operating. Another advantage is prop washes utilize the boat engine and propeller for thrust so extra equipment is kept to a minimum.

While the reader may correctly envision a 100 foot salvage vessel with massive ducts fitted over the props, much smaller versions can be constructed. A PVC or air conditioning elbow firmly mounted over an outboard motor propeller can achieve marvelous results. While prop washes move a significant amount of sand, a great deal of care must be exercised since an arm sucked into a prop is as good as amputated.

124.

Diver Propulsion Vehicles (DPVs)

DPVs are a ready-made source of power which can be used to remove sand. While they're designed to pull a diver through the water, they can easily be turned around to blow sand away from a specific area. Like the water jet, the main problem is hanging on since the thrust is in one direction only. If at all possible, it is advantageous to prop yourself against a rock or brace the machine against a solid object to avoid an unexpected underwater voyage.

Battery life is the main concern when using a DPV. Unlike dredges which can simply be refilled with gas, batteries must be charged or replaced when they run low.

The Mud Squisher

On occasion, a diver will stumble across an area that is so littered with metal debris that a metal detector is useless. Such was the case when I dived next to an old dock which I knew had to have older coins and jewelry somewhere in the mud bottom, but cans, pop tops, bottle caps and everything else imaginable made detecting an impossible task.

After confronting the same situation several more times in the same year, I designed what is affectionately known as the *Finnern Mud Squisher*. The principle and construction of the Mud Squisher are simple if not downright embarrassing. Take a 3-5 gallon plastic bucket and drill 1/2" holes in the bottom. Cut out two sections of the sides, line with 1/2" galvanized screen and attach a lead weight to the bottom of the bucket. Cut a round piece of plywood that is slightly less in diameter than the bottom of the bucket, paint or seal the wood and attach a handle. Tie a rope from the bucket to the handle, making sure the line is long enough to reach the bottom of the bucket.

To operate a Mud Squisher simply shovel the bottom sediment or sand into the bucket. With the bucket about half-full, place the plywood "plunger" into the bucket and begin an up and down motion. The idea is the mud and sand are forced out of the bucket through the screen leaving larger objects in the bucket. Believe it or not, it actually works!

The "Mud Squisher" is both simple to construct and easy to use.

Salvors have occasionally come under attack from environmentalists and government agencies when excavating the ocean bottom. The arguments against excavation are, in my opinion, complete nonsense. One need only watch the ocean during a gale or hurricane, or view a river during the spring runoff to see a dredge or other device cannot come close to what nature does annually. But since nonsense is commonly a legislative imperative, there are numerous laws regarding excavation and it is just as imperative to check the local statutes before investing in any equipment.

CHAPTER 9.

Treasure Hunting
Equipment Maintenance

Preventative maintenance of equipment should be an integral and consistent discipline in underwater treasure hunting. Due to the hostile environment in which this type of hunting is performed, detectors and other tools will last a mere fraction of their designed life expectancy if it is ignored. The usual culprits of destruction are sand, salt, sun and the water itself. And, unfortunately, all four are in plentiful supply at most water hunting sites.

Whether you hunt an ocean beach, in rivers or a fresh water swimming hole, sand and grit will inevitably enter your equipment. The real danger from sand is its abrasive nature. It can literally grind away plastic, nylon, metal and almost anything else if given enough time. For this reason, all equipment requires rinsing after each use. But a quick dip under the hose will not adequately do the job.

Tiny particles of sand can penetrate every opening in a metal detector. The best way to ensure they are removed is by disassembling the detector shafts from the coil and control box and rinsing thoroughly with fresh water. Special attention should be given to the control knobs and any part that moves or slides against another surface.

The same process should be used on treasure scoops and any handle extensions. The handle sections and the scoop should be taken apart prior to cleaning. After a complete rinsing with fresh water, the parts should be allowed to dry before reassembling. As with all equipment, detectors and scoops should be dried in the shade and never left in direct sunlight for any length of time. Sunlight can dry out rubber seals and gaskets, and the internal electronics within a detector can become much hotter than it was designed to withstand.

After hunting in salt water or a lake with a high mineral or alkaline content, it is better to soak equipment in warm (not hot) fresh water prior to rinsing. This removes salt crystals and other deposits which can be corrosive to metals. A bathtub works well for this. But in the unlikely event your spouse says something like, "one more sandy bathtub and you're outa here," (not that I have any personal experience at this), a large plastic trash container works well for this purpose.

An easy way to construct a cleaning station is to purchase a large plastic trash can and mount a water faucet or valve on the side near the bottom. The faucet allows for easy drainage, saves the trash can from possible breakage from tipping to drain, and even irrigates the flower bed when strategically placed.

About every underwater metal detector utilizes O-rings for watertight integrity. On a day-to-day basis, O-rings require no maintenance. However, each time the detector or battery compartment is opened and the seal breached, a series of steps must be taken to reseal the unit. The first step is to clean the O-ring and both sides of the compartment completely. A clean cloth or tissue can be used and there should be no sand or particles remaining when this is completed. The next step is to inspect the O-ring. If there are any cracks or the O-ring appears dry and brittle, it should be replaced. If the O-ring is in good condition, the next step is to lubricate it with silicone grease. Re-greasing an O-ring does not require a tremendous amount of silicone, however care should be taken that all surfaces of the O-ring are covered uniformly and completely.

After the O-ring is clean and lubricated it should be reinstalled in position taking care it doesn't make contact with any other surface. If it is accidentally dropped on a work bench or floor, it should be cleaned again before installing. When reassembling a clear plastic housing, it should be tightened to the degree an obvious black seal has been produced by the O-ring. Care should be taken to make the seal without over-tightening. If snaps are utilized, both should be cinched down simultaneously rather than one, then the other. If your machine has two or more bolts to attach the compartment cover, they should be tightened slowly and evenly.

If you wear a wetsuit during treasure hunting it is imperative to rinse the suit after each use, with special attention given to the zippers. This is especially needed with nylon zippers since they can be sanded smooth relatively easily if ill-maintained. Like other equipment, soaking the suit is better than a quick rinsing and periodic use of a commercial wetsuit conditioner is a good idea to eliminate bacteria and odors.

After rinsing, the suit should be hung in an outside shady area to dry. Avoid using narrow hangers to dry or store wetsuits since stretching or creasing may result. It is best to use special wetsuit hangers which are at least three inches wide at the shoulders.

Drysuits may be rinsed in much the same way as wetsuits. However, when rinsing drysuits, avoid putting too much stress on the seals since they can tear relatively easily.

Wetsuit and drysuit zippers require periodic lubrication to operate properly. It is best to use silicone grease or bees wax for this purpose rather than an oil-based product. But be careful not to apply the lubricant in massive amounts since sand tends to stick to the lubricated surface rendering another problem to overcome. Also, some manufacturers suggest avoiding silicone products for lubricating drysuit zippers since they will prevent a repair patch from attaching to the suit if the lubricant is transferred to another area. If there are any questions regarding the best lubricant for your particular suit, consult the owner's manual or manufacturer.

Most other diving equipment, mask, fins, gloves, etc., can be soaked and rinsed in much the same manner as wet and dry suits with the exception of the regulator. A regulator demands special care to avoid water seeping into the first stage. To avoid this, the first rule is to make sure the first stage dust cap is properly in place when storing or rinsing. When dipping a regulator it is also wise to lower the second stage, depth gauge and all low-pressure hoses first keeping the first stage at a higher level. Also, make sure the purge valve is not accidentally pushed inward when soaking or rinsing. An open purge valve allows water to enter the low pressure hose and, thus, the first stage. Some divers prefer to mount their regulators on a tank after rinsing and push the purge several times just to ensure no water is remaining in a hose or first stage.

Another good way to soak a regulator is to attach the first stage to a tank and open the valve prior to placing it in warm water. In this way no water can seap into the first stage since it is under pressure.

Tanks are relatively easy to maintain by soaking and rinsing after each use. It is advantageous to remove the tank boot prior to rinsing simply to ensure all sand and salt are completely removed. It is also prudent to crack the valve to blow out any residual rinse water prior to installing a regulator or filling.

As is customary, regulators and tanks alike should be inspected annually. A V.I.P. on a tank and yearly servicing on a regulator is cheap insurance indeed. As required by law, all tanks should be hydro-tested every five years.

Buoyancy compensators should be soaked and rinsed like other equipment. But care should be taken to remove all salt residue from the inside of the bladder to eliminate a build up of salt crystals on the inside. These salt crystals can cut the bladder rendering it useless. The easiest way to remove salt water is to first drain the bladder then refill it one third full with warm tap water. Move the water rapidly throughout the bladder then drain. Taste the water as it drains. If any salt is present, repeat the process.

Regardless of how well you maintain your equipment, some corrosion will probably occur. Since most bolts, snaps, etc. used on metal detectors and underwater equipment are stainless steel, there should be little problem from corrosion on these surfaces. But some corrosion may occur on aluminum or steel surfaces once the protective coatings are worn or scratched.

Corrosion on aluminum can be recognized by a white, chalky substance called aluminum oxide. One advantage to this is once the corrosion occurs, it actually coats the surface which helps inhibit further corrosion. But by the time this takes place, a scoop handle, for example, may be permanently frozen in place. Removing aluminum oxide is a simple process and can be accomplished with either aluminum wool or fine-grit wet/dry sand paper. But care should be taken not to sand the finish off the adjacent, unaffected areas.

Rust on steel (iron oxide) is more damaging but the problem is limited to the few underwater tools made from steel. Sand scoops or rock picks constructed from steel can, and probably will, rust after submersion in water or if any applied protective coatings wear off. While this can be corrected by sand blasting and refinishing, it's a lot of work which is destined to need repeating. It's been my experience that rusty sand scoops work just about as well as new ones, so I simply try to limit the rust by rinsing with fresh water and drying the scoop after each use. Even with a little rust, steel scoops and rock picks provide good service for many years.

Another type of corrosion can occur from battery acid. Leaking batteries in a metal detector is a serious matter and the manufacturer should be consulted prior to beginning any restoration. However, if this is not feasible or if the problem is minor and limited to the battery contacts, acid corrosion can be repaired relatively easily. First, use a small wire brush or fine sandpaper to clean the battery contacts. Next, make a paste from baking soda and water and apply it to the affected area to neutralize the acid. After about 10 minutes, remove the paste and clean with fresh water and dry thoroughly.

The same process can be used if the corrosion was caused by salt water droplets in the battery housing. But again, the manufacturer should be consulted before commencing any work.

Some fittings, wetsuit zippers and clips are constructed from brass or chromed brass. While this material is relatively impervious to most conditions, corrosion can occur. Corrosion on brass appears greenish or turquoise. It can be removed on small parts by soaking them in a 50% solution of white vinegar (acetic acid) and water, then rinsing with fresh water. On items such as brass zippers, corrosion can be removed by dipping a toothbrush in vinegar and brushing, then rinsing with fresh water.

The manufacturer's maintenance guidelines in the owner's

manual are the best source of information for taking care of your particular equipment. Today's underwater treasure hunting and diving equipment is designed to withstand the hostile environment of salt and sea. By following the manufacturer's instructions and with proper maintenance, diving equipment, detectors and accessories alike should give many years of trouble-free operation.

CHAPTER 10.

Cleaning And Restoration

There is often a false assumption that the average diver can only discover treasures nominal in worth. In reality, nothing could be further from the truth. Extremely rare and valuable items are discovered regularly by treasure hunters. Keeping this in mind, the value and/or rarity of a discovery needs to be determined prior to any cleaning or restoration. The reasons for this are many but two in particular are critical. First, most of us don't have the professional equipment required to properly restore some items. If a find is priceless it would indeed be ill-advised to shine it with a wire brush. Second, some items should not be cleaned at all. Rare coins, for example, are often worth much more with a natural patina. Polishing may make them shiny and pretty, but worth much less. So before using any of the following techniques, identify, and if necessary have appraised, any item which may be of value. And if appropriate, have a professional conservator do the job.

Restoring and cleaning objects found beneath the water can be a complicated endeavor and there are about as many opinions as to the best methods as there are treasure hunters. The following are some of the methods which can be used both effectively and economically.

Coins

By far, coins are the most common treasures recovered underwater. The vast majority are usually clad coins but silver coins may be found in abundance at older sites. Almost all silver coins recovered from salt water will have, to some degree, a coating of silver sulphide. This appears black and can make coins almost unrecognizable. Since most of the clad coins are worth face value or, in the case of silver, their bullion value, cleaning in bulk can be advantageous.

The concept of a coin tumbler is simple. It is merely a cylinder with a waterproof lid which is turned by a small electric motor. To operate, just load the coins, aggregate (rocks), water and cleaning solution into the tumbler, close it up and turn it on. The coins perpetually tumble around the rocks which polish off any corrosion or particles.

There are a variety of tumblers on the market with special aggregate and cleaning solutions available for silver, clad and copper coins. Tumbling coins is a simple process but a few rules should be kept in mind.

It is wise to tumble silver coins separately from copper coins and likewise clad coins should be tumbled by themselves. This is to ensure coins of different metals don't stain or scratch one another. Coins should be checked frequently when tumbling. Many coins may clean in as little as 15 minutes while others may require 24 hours or more to remove more stubborn stains. Once a coin is clean it should be removed from the tumbler since there is no value in subjecting it to unnecessary abrasion. After removing a coin it should be rinsed with fresh water and dried to eliminate water stains or stains from the cleaning solution.

While there is always an air of excitement upon returning from a treasure hunting adventure with a pocketful of coins, it is wise to save up enough coins to run a full load. This saves electricity and also allows the tumbler to clean to its fullest potential since the coins themselves provide some of the abrasion. But be cautious not to overload the cylinder since movement of the items would then be restricted.

There are times when a coin is found which is not a key date that requires professional cleaning, yet is indeed valuable due

The author displays a steamship luggage tag darkened beyond recognition from 100 years under the sea (top). Below is the same tag after polishing. The dishes are from the same steamship company.

135.

to its age, history or just personally. In this case tumbling is an overkill. There are a variety of cleaning products on the market which do a fine job of cleaning without the use of abrasives.

One favored method utilizes Tarn-X, a cleaning solution available at many retail stores. Simply wrap the silver coin in aluminum foil and place it in a small dish filled with Tarn-X. The initial cleaning can occur fairly rapidly so the coin should be checked every few minutes or so. Each time the coin is unwrapped and checked, lightly wipe the surface with a cotton ball. When the desired effect is accomplished, clean the coin with fresh water and dry. This method works well since there is little actual contact with the coin so scratching is almost nonexistent.

Brass

Brass items are found regularly underwater and can range from antiquated toys to shipwreck relics. And although brass usually exits the water a dirty brown/green color, it can be polished to a golden luster with a little effort.

The first step is to dip the piece in muriatic acid if any barnacles or sea growth are present, then rinse with fresh water immediately following the acid dip. This process will clean the surface of any organic growth but be extremely careful to adhere to the directions and warnings on the acid bottle. Muriatic acid can eat away other things as well.

After cleaning the growth and rinsing off the acid, the next step is the initial polishing. The fastest way to accomplish this is with a fine wire wheel on a high-speed drill motor or, on finer pieces, a polishing/buffing wheel. Simply buff the piece making sure not to focus on any one area for too long a period.

When polishing brass, it is commonplace to shine it to a copper color before the golden color appears. This is especially the case in pieces which have been submerged underwater for a long time. And once in a while, a piece recovered from the ocean will not return to the golden sheen due to the salt water leaching out the zinc. But keep trying until you're absolutely sure it refuses to turn golden.

After using the wire wheel, the next step is to hand buff the

Even older brass objects can be cleaned and polished to like-new condition.

piece using a common brass cleaner such as Brasso or jeweler's rouge and a soft cloth. This can take awhile. At first the buffing cloth will continually turn black. You're not finished until it no longer turns black, or you're about to drop from exhaustion.

While the item will shine like new after polishing, it will not remain so for very long. Brass tarnishes fairly fast. To eliminate this, a spray coating of urethane, lacquer or epoxy resin will protect the finish for many years.

In the event a brass item is found that was once made to operate, such as a hinge, one way to free the object from corrosion is by soaking it in white vinegar (acetic acid) prior to any other treatment. This literally neutralizes the corrosion although it may take awhile.

Iron

Iron can be recognized as black in color when discovered underwater whereas steel is usually orange. Steel corrodes much faster than iron when submerged in salt water, however the restoration treatment of both metals is the same.

Iron items recovered from fresh water usually fare well with just a little cleaning or light polishing. Not so with iron items recovered from salt water. A relic which has been submerged in salt water for many years actually absorbs the salt which binds with the corrosive iron particles to form ferric chlorides. If the piece were to be removed from the sea and dried without treatment, the salts would crystallize and the piece would simply crumble.

To prevent this, the first thing one does after recovering an iron relic from the ocean is to bring it home in a plastic bag filled with salt water. This eliminates some of the immediate deterioration which can take place from exposure to oxygen.

Electrolytic Reduction

Salvors and archaeologists alike utilize electrolytic reduction for the preservation of most metals. This method is sometimes referred to as reverse electrolysis however this is somewhat of a misnomer since it indicates the treatment will restore metal that has corroded away, which it will not.

To restore an iron object, you will need a plastic or glass tank of sufficient size, a D.C. battery charger preferably with a variable transformer, alligator clips, two pieces of stainless steel, water, wire and electrolyte which for iron is sodium hydroxide (caustic soda).

To create the electrolytic cell, simply place the iron object in the tank. Inset two stainless steel sheets, one at each end of the tank, and connect the positive wires via alligator clips to the top of the metal sheets. Fill the tank with a 5% solution of caustic soda (make sure appropriate gloves and a face shield are worn when utilizing this or any chemicals). Connect the negative poles to the iron object and plug in the charger.

In this process the stainless steel is the anode and the iron

Most metal objects recovered require some type of restoration treatment.

object is the cathode. Low amperage, usually 2-10 amps, is preferred when setting up electrolytic reduction system. This will cause small bubbles to form on the relic but if a massive amount of bubbles appear, reduce the amperage.

As the process continues a black residue will form. This should be cleaned off periodically. Small pieces may take a couple of weeks to complete while larger pieces may take a year or more.

Upon completion the piece must be thoroughly cleaned and placed back into the tank, this time the amperage is applied in fresh water only. After cleaning and drying, a finish coat of paint or clear acrylic spray finish can then be applied.

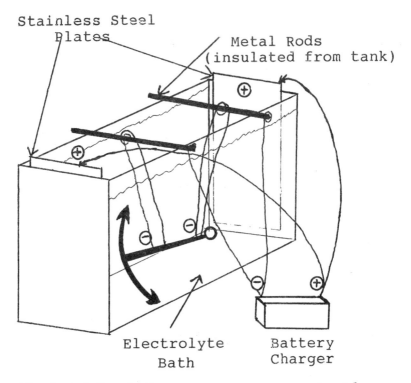

Stainless Steel Plates

Metal Rods (insulated from tank)

Electrolyte Bath

Battery Charger

The electrolytic reduction process can preserve most metals.

The same process can be used for metals other than iron or steel. For silver coins, for example, use the same tank and stainless steel anode. But this time place the relics on a copper mesh cathode and use a 5% solution of formic acid for the electrolyte. The negative poles are attached directly to the copper mesh in this instance.

Wood

Like iron, wood recovered from salt water contains salt crystals. But unlike iron, these crystals actually support the cell walls of the wood so a fresh water bath isn't necessary or advised. Again, deterioration begins the minute the item is removed from the water so it must be placed in a bag filled with water immediately upon surfacing.

Wood can be preserved by several techniques. One of the more common methods is a six month soak in polyethylene glycol. This is the method most shipwreck salvors employ. If a piece has not been down too long, soaking for a month or so in teak oil may suffice as well.

CHAPTER 11.

Reading Nautical Charts

Nautical charts have been used by seafarers for centuries to navigate for short distances or around the world. Charts are useful in treasure hunting by identifying a specific area which has been researched or even for seeking a likely spot to try your luck.

The common chart used today is called a Mercator Projection, named for its inventor, 16th century cartographer Gerardus Mercator. The Mercator Projection simplifies the primary problem in accurate chart making; how do you fit a round earth on a flat piece of paper? To accomplish this, Gerardus used lines in the shape of a cylinder and wrapped them around the globe. The vertical lines are called meridians of longitude and represent planes through the earth intersecting

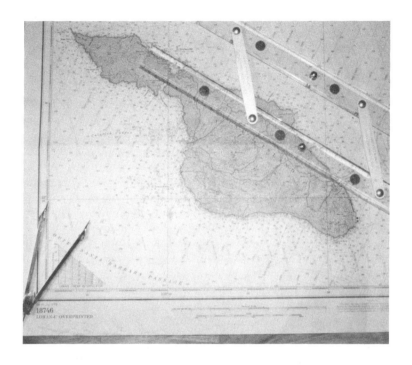

The latitude scales border the sides of a chart whereas the longitude scales border the top and bottom.

each pole. These lines are used for measuring distances east and west from a specific plane called the prime meridian which passes through Greenwich, England, totaling 360 degrees (180 degrees west and east from the prime meridian). The horizontal lines are called parallels of latitude and measure north and south beginning at latitude 0 (the Equator) to 90 degrees at either pole.

Latitude measurements (commonly abbreviated Lat.) are always written with N or S to designate north or south of the Equator. In the same fashion, longitude (abbreviated Long.) is always accompanied by E or W to designate whether it's east or west of the longitude 0.

Unlike land maps which use miles or kilometers for reference, charts utilize degrees, minutes and seconds. One degree is equal to 60 nautical miles, one minute is equal to one nautical mile, a second is one tenth of a nautical mile. The perfection of this system is apparent when we understand the circumference of the earth is about 21,600 nautical miles, the equivalent of 360 degrees.

The latitude scale borders the sides of nautical charts while the longitude scales border the top and bottom. Both scales represent degrees however all measurements for nautical miles are performed on the latitude (side) scales only.

While this may sound complicated, it's very simple in application. The term "coordinates" is used to designate a specific place on the earth. The coordinates of any location must include both latitude and longitude in degrees, minutes and seconds with the latitude always being the first figure listed.

It's the coordinates of a location that is of primary interest to treasure hunters. Let's say you've stumbled upon the only known chart marking the location of the ultimate sunken treasure of all time. It's hand-drawn with incredible detail but the author left out a few items. He also forgot to label any of the land masses on the chart leaving you with no idea if that's New York or Tasmania. But in the corner is faintly written, L 33°27'.8N, Lo 118°29'.3W.

By just looking at the above coordinates we can see our site is in the northern hemisphere (N) and it's a long way west of Greenwich, England. (If you wanted to know exactly how far you could simply figure $118 \times 60 + 29.3$ = nautical miles west from the meridian on which Greenwich is located). But there is an easier way.

Charts are available in various scales. Since you're still at the stage of trying to identify a general location, a small scale chart would be in order, probably one in the 1:1,000,000 scale range. These charts are usually reserved for ocean going vessels since little detail is given but a large expanse is represented. But as the geographic area is narrowed, a larger scale chart can be used. Typical small-craft charts are 1:80,000-1:40,000 in scale, but charts of bays and inlets can be 1:10,000 scale.

The first thing one notices when looking at a chart is the top is always true north (the compass rose also designates magnetic north). By looking at the side scale for latitude and the bottom scale for longitude we can clearly see the intersection of latitude 33° and longitude 118° is not near Tasmania or New York but

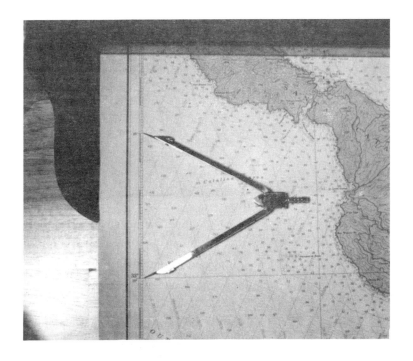

A T-square can be used to line up coordinates.

rather somewhere around California.

It isn't long before we realize we need a chart of the San Pedro Channel located in the southern portion of California (in this case N.O.A.A. Chart #18746). As we unfold the chart (never roll charts since they become unmanageable) we can easily see the general area where the "ultimate treasure" is located, but to narrow the exact location we must use instruments.

To find the longitude we simply look at the bottom scale and find 118°. Next to the larger degree markings we see smaller numbers representing minutes. We then find the closest number to 29', which in this case is 30'. The minute scale is marked every five minutes then further broken down into individual minutes and seconds (remember, each minute is equal to one nautical mile). To find our correct longitude, we simply count back from 30' one nautical mile to 29' and add the 3 seconds

145.

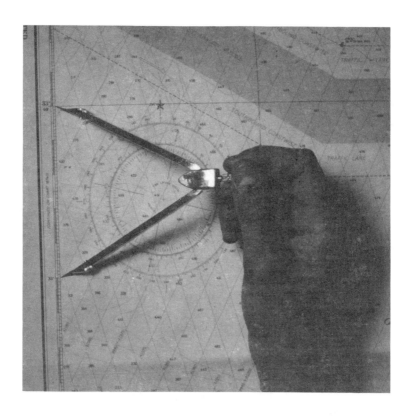

Dividers can be used to measure any distance by using the latitude scales of a chart. Here, they establish the distance of five nautical miles.

using the second scale. If preferred, this could be done from the 25' mark by counting upward to 29'.3.

After locating our longitude we mark this with pencil then take a standard drafting T-square and line it up on our mark. We then draw a light line at the approximate intersection of the latitude we're to seek next.

To find the latitude we repeat the exact same process using the side scale. When we place our T-square on our latitude mark, the intersection of the T-square and our previously drawn longitude line is the exact location of the ultimate treasure. After drawing a pencil line at the intersection it's simple to see that literally "X" marks the spot.

While knowing the location is helpful, more information is required to understand its relativity to other land masses. Mileage is determined with the aid of dividers. To use them, we draw a line from a specific point on the chart to the plotted coordinates. Our starting point would normally be the harbor from which we plan to embark. We take our dividers and spread the pointed ends apart and place them on the latitude scale and adjust the points until they equal five minutes. (For small measurements one would probably use one minute and conversely 10 minutes for larger measurements).

Keeping in mind five minutes equal five nautical miles, we place one point of the dividers at the beginning of our line and simply walk the other point around until it meets our line. We repeat the process counting the five mile increments until the remaining distance is less than five miles. We then measure that distance with the dividers, place them on the latitude scale and measure the remaining distance. Hence, we know the exact distance from any place we choose.

Most certainly plotting and measuring are only a small part of piloting and navigation and a full course must be completed prior to firing up a boat engine. But charts can give us much more information than just the coordinates of a specific location. Charts are literally warehouses of information. Most charts contain symbols and/or abbreviations designating obstructions, shipwrecks, rocks, types of coastlines and bottom topography just to name a few of the features. The following graphs list some of the more pertinent abbreviations of interest to treasure hunters. For a complete list of symbols, books are available from N.O.A.A. or your local marine hardware store.

Shipwrecks And Obstructions

Wreckage, Wks, Wk......................Shipwreck or wreckage
(Shipwrecks can also be denoted by symbols including a silhouette of a sinking ship or a horizontal line with three intersecting and smaller vertical lines. A shipwreck symbol may be followed by PA which indicates the position is approximate.)

Subm piles, Subm piling................Submerged piling(s)
(Abbreviations can be accompanied by small circles designating the pilings or, a circle followed by a dashed line followed by another circle).

Types Of Bottoms

Grd......Ground	Sn..........Shingle
S........Sand	P.............Pebbles
M........Mud or muddy	St.............Stones
Oz.......Ooze	Rk,rky......Rocks
Ml.......Marl	Blds......Boulders
Cl.......Clay	Ck.............Chalk
G........Gravel	Ca.....Calcareous
Qz.......Quartz	Sh.............Shells
Co.......Coral	Oys........Oysters
Co Hd....Coral Head	Ms.........Mussels
Vol......Volcanic	Spg........Sponge
Vol Ash..Volcanic Ash	K..............Kelp
La.......Lava	Wd......Seaweed
Pm.......Pumice	Grs............Grass
fne......Fine	spk......Speckled
crs......Course	gty...........Gritty
sft......Soft	dec......Decayed
hrd......Hard	vard........Varied
stf......Stiff	unev......Uneven
grd.....Ground(shells)	stk............sticky

Tides And Currents

HW.......High water
HHW......Higher high water
LW.......Low water
LLW......Lower low water
MTL......Mean tide level
MSL......Mean sea level
Str......Stream
ht.......Height
Sp.......Spring tide
Np.......Neap tide
MHW.......Mean high water
MHHW.......Mean higher water
MLW.......Mean low water
Vel.......Velocity
kn.......Knot

Miscellaneous Abbreviations

Subm ruins......Submerged ruins
Anch............Anchorage
Hbr.............Harbor
P...............Port

Whf......Wharf
Lng......Landing
Hn.......Haven
Hk.......Hulk
(wreck)

EPILOGUE

Underwater treasure hunting transcends many facets of diving, oceanography and exploration technology and it's simply not possible to cover all aspects in a limited space. I can only hope this book is but a first step to further research and study. There are indeed millions of dollars worth of treasure trapped beneath the waters of the world just awaiting discovery, and most certainly you are capable of that treasured moment when it sees the light of day for the first time since its loss.

But while treasure may be the entity for which we search, it would indeed be a tragedy to be so focused that the pleasures of the hunt are missed. There's an incomparable exhilaration in the anticipation of finding sunken treasure that should be enjoyed and relished. Some of the most enjoyable days I've spent in the outdoors have not been financially productive yet they were rewarding none the less. And quite possibly the friends I've made along the way and the sights I've seen are really the greatest treasures after all.

It is truly unfortunate that some individuals view treasure hunting negatively. I suppose this is merely another bizarre sign of the times in which we live, but the fact remains there are those who perpetually attempt to pass legislation to curtail the activity or place sites off-limits despite public outcry. There have been ridiculous judgments and laws passed in the last few years which are counterproductive to just about everyone involved. Yet despite the absurdity, this band of individuals persist. They believe all man-made objects under the sea should belong to governments, and individuals should have no right to explore or salvage them. It is their quest to literally own the past. They believe it is *their* heritage, not *our* heritage.

As you enter the realm of treasure hunting, I believe it is a responsibility to make your opinions known to lawmakers and elected representatives. But it is also the responsibility of every treasure hunter to make sure there is no ammunition to argue in favor of such legislation. Private property is to be respected, laws are to be understood and obeyed whether or not you agree with them, fill all excavations and leave no trace of your passing. In this way, we will leave a legacy for future generations; we will ensure they, too, will be able to dream a most universal reverie, and experience firsthand the thrill of discovering sunken treasure.

Good hunting!

TREASURE LOG

TREASURE LOG

TREASURE LOG